G'day ya Pommie b......!

G'day ya Pommie b.....!

and other
cricketing memories

David Lloyd

Illustrated by
Colin Whittock

WEIDENFELD & NICOLSON
London

First published in Great Britain in 1992 by
Weidenfeld and Nicolson
The Orion Publishing Group
Orion House
5 Upper St Martin's Lane
London WC2H 9EA

A catalogue reference is available from
the British Library

ISBN 0 297 81279 3

Produced by Lennard Books
Mackerye End, Harpenden
Herts AL5 5DR

Designed by Cooper Wilson
in associaton with Forest Publications
Jacket origination by Amega Litho

Printed and bound in Slovenia

Contents

Introduction

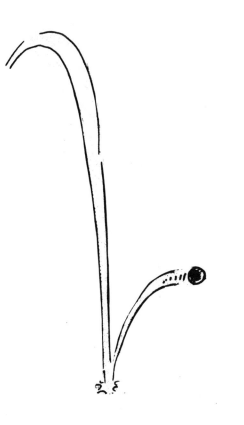

Player – Umpire – Broadcaster

Poacher turned gamekeeper was certainly true when I retired from first-class cricket in 1983, took a year off, and then applied to join the umpires list in 1985. Most of the lads on the list are ex-pros, they 'know the ropes'. Picking the seam, lip-ice on the ball, gamesmanship, bad light, nicked it and stood – we have all seen it, done it, been there.

There are a couple of meetings to attend at Lord's before getting out in the middle at the start of the season. All the bizarre incidents from last season are talked about.

"It came on raining at 4.55 pm on the last day just before the statutory 20 overs. They were behind on the quota of overs for the day but play resumed at 5.08 pm – how many overs of the last 20 had been lost?"

The Grimsby fish man, Don Oslear, would know. And he did. His oratory blinded everyone with science, but he knew. Is this still the job for me? I thought we just counted to six and gave 'em out from time to time. After that meeting I realized that I had played for nearly 20 years and knew nowt about the game!

The next three years were perhaps the most enjoyable I have had in the game. Colleagues were very helpful, games were hard with plenty to think about, and players were players.

I don't know what I had done to deserve my first fixture, Cambridge University versus Essex. They would all be there, Lever, Pont, East, Hardie and the like. Something was bound to happen. Essex fielded first, Lever came in from my end, slow half-volley, straight onto the bat, smack – the thing disintegrated – it was an orange!

Essex again, this time against Somerset at Taunton. We had done all the preliminaries, checked the wicket, gauged the balls, etc. There was no boundary rope or line, so the

advertising boards were the boundary. No problem.
Regulations state that if the ball hits the board full on, it is
four. It has to clear the board for six. But, and this is the sting
in the tail, the fielder can lean against the board to complete a
catch. Got it!

David East, the Essex wicket-keeper, is batting. He gets a
bouncer which he hooks brilliantly to deep square leg. Great
shot. Hang on, Jon Hardy is under it, he leans on the board,
arms aloft, takes the catch ... and the board falls over with
Hardy sat on it! Why me? Decision? Out. Exit one unhappy
East.

Still at Taunton, this time Somerset against Middlesex in the
Sunday League. The game is on TV. Three balls to go, I.T.
Botham on strike, twelve to win. Wayne 'Diamond' Daniel is
purveying from my end. 'Both' stops him in his run-up, prods
the pitch a couple of times and says to me:

WHAT A JAFFA!

"Who you backing?"

I reply: "Three to go, twelve to win is a good contest. Is there any chance of getting on with it because 'Songs of Praise' is on next and we're running a little late?"

The first of the three is a 70 mph low full-toss, delivered from wide of the crease which Both hits into the car park. Two to go, six to win. He blocks the next one on purpose, just to get the crowd on the edge of their seats. The game stops, 'Gatt', 'Embers' and Wayne gather at mid-off. 'Philippe Henri' comes across to join them, wife and fielders were moved everywhere. At last, everyone is in position. 'Diamond' steams in. It is a similar delivery to the first. It gets a similar response.

The ball was last seen disappearing over the scoreboard. The crowd went mad. I was just pulling up stumps at my end when a bat clouted me across the backside. Both again.

"You stick with me, pal, I'll make you famous!" he said.

Happy days, great times. Now I am into something different. Broadcasting. And I start off in that as the young apprentice. Some Test Match Special work and some BSB satellite TV.

Yes, Johners has offered me the biggest slice of chocolate fudge cake which I eagerly accept. One mouthful into it, he immediately asks me about the technicalities of away-swing bowling from close to the wicket. Much mirth and guffaws all round. I know Jonners promotes the Primary Club tie for batsman who have been out first ball. Pehaps he should strike one for all the summarisers who have fallen for the chocolate cake routine.

Lots of letters, too. Some complimentary and some not so. For instance Peter Baxter, the producer, received one which was very short and to the point, written on the back of a National Savings Certificate paying-in slip. It said:

"Why don't you get shot of that biased Lancashire b....." I can only assume he meant me and not Farokh Engineer. By the way, the postmark was Wakefield.

It is not all cricket either. During the Old Trafford Test

match I was on with Christopher Martin-Jenkins when it started to rain. CMJ offered that "at least it would do the gardens good". I agreed enthusiastically, which prompted him to ask if I was a keen gardener.

"Not really," I replied "but I have just put a pond in."

"Oh, do you have any fish in it?" he enquired.

"Yes, and a fair amount of algae," I said.

Fred Trueman chipped in from behind that:

"I should be wary of herons if you have fish about."

"I don't think there are many herons in Accrington," I said.

"Oh yes there are," said our first caller. "There are two on the canal bank at Oswaldwistle."

Thank you. Our next caller offered very interesting advice on the dispersal of algae and another was a noted authority on Koi carp, who would be only too pleased to come to my home and advise me on the welfare and general well-being of the fish. I really did not have the heart to say that it is only a six by four pool liner and the goldfish are from the local fair. Perhaps this puts the record straight.

Playing Days

THE OLD ENEMY

An Aussie Tour is different. They are the Old Enemy, just like Lancashire versus Yorkshire, Middlesex versus Surrey or Warwickshire versus Worcestershire but on a much grander scale. After all, we sent them there in the first place!

An affectionate welcome

In 1974 when I was first-timer on my one and only tour, I obviously looked forward to the experience with great anticipation. It was when we finally arrived and were going through the usual immigration routine that I had an inkling that the general public were going to be less than friendly towards us.

There was no: "Hi, lovely to see you, have an enjoyable stay in Australia," from a courteous passport official.

No, it was: "G'day, ya Pommie b......., come over for another good hiding, have ya?"

Tony Greig assured me that 'ya Pommie b......' was really a sign of affection. I was not convinced.

There were, of course, many official functions to attend. A chance to meet new friends and interesting people. John Edrich and Fred Titmus would always arrive last. They had been before.

There were also standard questions asked by our 'new friends'.

"G'day, ya Pommie b......, what do you think of our Sheelaghs, what do you think of our sea, what do you think of our sun?"

There were also standard answers.

"Yes, there are no ladies in England, the sea is miles away, and I do beg your pardon, but what is the sun?"

The Australian cricket connoisseur would also attend these

functions and after the inevitable one-way introduction would ask the very perceptive question:

"Can ya hook?"

Before you could get any sort of reply out he would always come back with:

"Good for you, mate, 'cos when Thommo gets going you'll need plenty of practice."

An Australian welcome

Have you heard the one about the Australian Rules Ladies Football presentation evening when the Master of Ceremonies said:

"In the audience tonight we have members of the England cricket team. I hope all you ladies give them the clap that they deserve!"

The wit of Jeff Thomson

Thommo was a great fast bowler for a relatively short period of time. A very easy approach, javelin thrower's action and searing pace. He will, I am sure, be remembered for his one and only quote;

"I love to see blood on the wicket."

I recall thinking at the time, as I was the opening batsman, that he meant mine and not his. All very disconcerting for this son of Accrington, renowned for his cover drive.

A difference in interpretation

I mention that Thommo was exceptionally pacey, particularly in Australia, but not so in England. Over here he had to contend with the great Test Match umpires, like Tommy Spencer. Tommy knew that 'if he is on the line, he's mine'. Thommo's first over in England went into double figures in terms of deliveries. Tommy had him.

A bit different over there. I remember mentioning in the dressing room after a particularly long and hostile spell from

Thommo that he was over the front line and, therefore, no-balling for the majority of deliveries. I was encouraged to point this out to the umpire after the break. I thought I did this quite tactfully in saying to the umpire that:

"He gets quite close, doesn't he, sir?"

There were, in fact, no foot markings behind the front line.

The umpire replied, "He's close enough. Anyway, we don't agree with that law over here."

I couldn't resist it. It just came out.

"You do when we're bowling," I said.

A painful introduction

The wicket at Perth is like lightning. I should know, it was there that I first faced Jeff Thomson. Thommo hit me with what the press usually says is 'a blow in the groin.' My abdominal protector was completely inverted. It hurt. I was assisted from the field and took no further part in the day's proceedings.

The following morning I was still feeling one below par, so to speak, and asked Mike Denness when he would like me to bat. He said, "Next."

Our two lads went out to resume the innings as I settled into a corner of the dressing room to get mentally prepared. After two minutes there was a terrific sustained roar. I deduced that we hadn't hit a six. Out I went. Will it be bouncer or yorker? Whatever it was it hit me straight in the throat and I went down for another compulsory eight count. Thommo retrieved the ball from my feet, looked me straight in the eye and we both said in unison, "G'day ya Pommie b......!" Always remember, all you future tourists, this is a term of affection.

It always pays to be friendly

Thommo has been well documented but our chaps can rest assured whenever they go out there the Aussies will find a new one. They always do. Thomson, Pascoe, Hogg, Hughes,

McDermott. Yes, there will always be another one out there.

It is always best to get these quickies on your side. Pass the time of day with them and generally be pleasant especially if you are an opening batsman. It works. The third Test on the 1974/75 tour was at Sydney and everything had been going well. No broken bones or fatal injuries. In fact the game was played in a jolly good spirit – until Dennis Lillee came in to bat.

Dennis had given us a rough time in the previous two Tests and so I started to chat to him to get him in a favourable mood for when it was our turn to bat.

The usual things like:"How's the wife?" and "Good luck Dennis, enjoy your knock."

Tony Greig obviously wasn't seeing the situation as I was and bowled him a bouncer first ball, which struck him on the point of the elbow. I immediately asked Dennis if he was OK, and pointed out that I thought that the ball had jumped up from a good length.

Keith Fletcher, fielding at gully shouted in that Eastenders' accent:

"Well done, Greigy, give 'im another."

The atmosphere of the game suddenly changed. Lillee

reared round and said:

"Who said that?"

"I did," said Fletch defiantly.

We finished the day's play and retired to our hotel. We were all together in the 'team room' watching the News when an interview with Dennis Lillee came onto the screen. Now, as England players, we were not allowed to give interviews during a game but it seemed that all the Aussie players had their own programmes

It was either the 'Ian Chappell Show' or the 'Jeff Thomson Show' or the 'Rod Marsh Show'. This one was certain to be the 'Dennis Lillee Show'.

After all the usual questions about the game in progress, Lillee was asked:

"How do you get on with the England team, what sort of blokes are they?"

"The Poms are good sorts," he replied. "I get on well with them all."

He then leaned forward and looking straight to camera continued:

"Except that little weasel, Fletcher. I know you are watching and I will sort you out tomorrow."

18

We all had a good laugh about it, but it was not so funny if you happened to be Keith Fletcher.

The next day Australia made inroads into our batting and the moment of truth arrived when Fletch had to go out and bat. No helmet, no visor, just his MCC cap with St George on his horse as the badge. Lillee met him at the gate and escorted him to the middle.

"Now it's my turn, ya Pommie b......"

It was as if all Australia had heard the interview. There was a tremendous crescendo of noise around the ground. Lillee 'threw the kitchen sink' at him, as it were, but Fletch was very watchful and played superbly well. Then it happened, that one false move that a batsman never wants to make. Lillee bowled another bouncer which did not get up as much as Fletch anticipated and it hit him straight on the head as he took his eye off the ball.

We had all been watching proceedings on the edge of our seats in the dressing room and I will never forget Geoff Arnold, the former Surrey and England fast bowler, jumping up and shouting:

"Blimey, he's just knocked St George off his 'orse!"

Aussie spectators have long memories
It's not only fast bowlers who like to get even. In 1974 John Snow was over doing some TV commentary work. The Aussies remembered him as the villain of Ray Illingworth's previously victorious team. He was working high up in the commentary box at Perth when the local punters literally tried to take the

scaffolding down. I don't think that they wanted to shake hands with him. He looked absolutely petrified. That same term of affection kept cropping up. "Come down, ya Pommie b......! "

Nothing changes at Immigration

Getting to Australia is a doddle these days. 24 hours and you are there. Invariably, you will get delayed in Hong Kong for eight hours or so, and I have heard it rumoured that this can be quite a pleasurable experience. You may leave Hong Kong, it is said, with more than you went in with but at least you enjoyed it.

I went out at the end of the last Test series that England played out there in 1990/91. We were well and truly beaten by the time I arrived for the final Test at Perth, and the Aussies can tell a Pommie when he is down from a mile away. As lots of you know it should be plain sailing getting through Immigration. I say, it *should* be. In Australia you have to get past the rather strict Immigration official, who, it has to be said, is not the brightest. As dim as a Toc-H lamp, more like.

You still don't get a warm: "Welcome to Australia Mr. Lloyd, are you here for the cricket, do enjoy your stay".

Instead there's that familiar greeting: "G'day ya pommie b......., here for the cricket? We've given you another good hiding".

Now, he holds the cards, he has the aces. You have to smile meekly at the man as I did, thinking to myself, 'C'mon let me in. I could do with a bath, a drink and I really do want to go to sleep'.

He will not let you until he has told you every joke that's going the rounds about the England cricket team. Starting with:

"Have you heard about the Aussie Sheelagh who has accused one of the England batsmen of rape? The judge asked 'How do you know he was one of the England batsmen?' The Sheelagh replied 'Because he wasn't in very long'."

He quickly followed this with:

"I suppose you know the definition of optimism."

I said "No, but I'm sure you're going to tell me."

"Yes," he said, "that's an England batsman going out with sun cream on."

He went on and on. I was livid but, of course, you have to keep chuckling along. Eventually he finished and said:

"OK mate, good on ya sport, you can come in now."

By this time I was seething and thought 'he's not getting away with that'. I knew he was not the brightest so I took a photograph out of my jacket pocket and said to him:

"You obviously love your cricket; take a look at this. It's a picture of one of the England boys. I know he is sat in his pram, is probably about fifteen months old and has a dummy in his mouth, but I'm sure you'll recognise him."

The immigration officer studied the picture and quickly declared:

"That's David Gower."

I said, "It's not Gower."

"Gooch?" he suggested.

"Not Gooch," I replied.

"Lamb?"

"No."

"Atherton?"

"No," I said. "Do you give in?"

"Yes," he said. "Who is it?"

"That's Devon Malcolm," I said.

I told you they were dim!

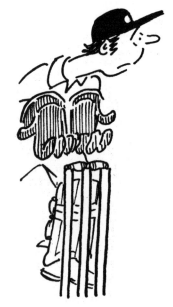

THE MANAGEMENT

Alec Bedser

When I first played Test cricket, the England manager, or
chairman of selectors, was Alec Bedser. Alec and I got on really
well and we had some good fun together. He could get very
serious though, and on one occasion during a team talk he
mentioned that our quickies – Bob Willis, Mike Hendrick,
Geoff Arnold, Chris Old and Peter Lever – always seemed to be
carrying minor injuries. He went on to say:

"I never used to get injured. I used to get fit by bowling.
Bowling a lot gets you fit. I used to bowl 45 overs every day. I
got bowling fit."

I couldn't resist chipping in with:

"You can't have been bowling so well, then, if you had to
keep bowling 45 overs every day. Couldn't you get anyone
out?" The look on his face said it all as he was totally
flabbergasted.

"Here, hey, what do you mean?"

Then there was a pause as he twigged what was happening.
A broad grin appeared on his face, as he said:

"You're winding me up aren't you?"

Come on, manager, would I do that?

Short and sweet

When we got to Australia, Alec was the spokesman who would
respond on behalf of the team at dinners and official functions.
He had one cracking story which was his finale to every speech
he made around Australia. We heard it so often that at the end
we all used to join in the punch line. It went something like
this.

The Duke of Norfolk had a racehorse trained by a chap
called Sid Furnell. Sid used to send detailed reports to His

Grace about how the horse was progressing – its training routine, diet sheets, time trials, etc. The Duke contacted Sid and asked him to be more precise explaining that he was a very busy man and did not have time to read all the reports that Sid was sending. All he needed was a short note informing him of how the horse had gone on in its race.

The horse ran and the Duke received a very obscure telegram which just read: S.F. – S.F. – S.F. – S.F.

The only S.F. that the Duke knew was Sid Furnell and so he gave him a ring and asked him about the telegram. Sid confirmed that it was from him and that it was a report of the horse's last race.

"But what does it all mean?" asked the Duke.

Sid explained.

"Started, farted, slipped and fell, see you Friday, Sid Furnell."

A natural method

The Norfolks are the leading Catholic family in England and another story attributed to the Duke is that he apparently said that it was a great pity that the West Indians had all the grace, movement and natural rhythm, when the people who really needed it were the Catholics.

The modern approach

A lot has been said about the fitness and track suit regime of Messrs Gooch and Stewart. On top of all that the England boys have psychology sessions and intelligence tests and they also have a resident padre, the Reverend Andrew Wingfield-Digby.

At the intelligence test Micky Stewart asks the questions and when big 'Syd' Lawrence was put through his paces, Micky asked him:

"What is pink, twelve inches long and hangs out of a man's pyjamas?"

"His foot," said Syd.

"Correct," said 'Bamber' Stewart.

"Question two," Micky went on. "Where do women have short black curly hair?"

"Africa," said Syd, quick as a flash.

"Now then," said Micky, "question three is much harder and you can nominate any member of the team to help you."

Syd looked round the room and said:

"I'll have the Rev. I'll have Wingers-Dingers."

The Reverend looked rather sheepish before saying,

"It's no use asking me, I got the first two wrong!"

OK, OK, so it's a joke!

TALES FROM THE COUNTY CIRCUIT

From the bowler's point of view

Bob Wincer was an opening bowler with Derbyshire and, after the close of play in a game against Lancashire at Liverpool, he was recounting the day's proceedings. In particular, he recalled the first over he had bowled at Clive Lloyd.

"I knew he had been 'out of nick' recently and so I made a conscious effort to make him play at every ball. The first one pitched off-stump and came back a little and he just got his bat down in time. I hit him on the pad with the next ball and the third flew over the top of the stumps. He played and missed at the next couple and I thought, this is it, the last ball of the over, he is mine for the taking. I bowled it a little wider and well pitched up, looking for the edge to slip. He came onto the front foot – and pinched a six off me!"

Just one of those days

In the same game at Liverpool, Fred Swarbrook, the Derbyshire left-arm spinner, was having a particularly bad time. It seems to be a quirk of the game that left-arm spinners periodically 'lose it'. It has certainly happened to quite a number that I can remember – Phil Edmonds, Maninder Singh, Don Wilson, to name but three. Anyway, Fred had had some sort of medical help by way of hypnotherapy or a faith healer. Someone in that field had told him that, before he came on to bowl, he had to rub a pebble that she had given him, and that this would give him confidence.

The captain gave Fred the nod that he wanted him to bowl. So out came the pebble and Fred went through his routine. The poor lad bowled dreadfully, and here was a chap who had taken nine wickets in an innings in a first-class match. He was obviously a good bowler but he had just lost it.

Things got worse, head-high full tosses, double-bouncers, wides. Everything was coming down. I am sure everyone felt sorry for Fred, who was obviously very embarrassed by it all. It needed a touch of humour. David Steele supplied it. He was fielding at silly mid off and, turning to Fred, said:

"Fred, lad. Have you ever thought of bowling the pebble?"

A perfect understanding

Norman Hill and Brian Bolus were a very eccentric pair of opening batsmen at Nottingham. For a start Norman weighed in at about 18 stone. They did not have that crisp, "Yes, No, Wait" calling routine that most batsmen have.

"Should we have one there, Nimble?" Bolus would call to Norman.

"I think there may be more, Bol," Norman would reply.

"Yes, several, I think," from 'Bol'.

One year we played on Old Trafford without a boundary rope and using the whole arena. The Notts fixture was played on the pavilion side of the square which meant that the boundary on the popular side was massive. Sure enough Bolus hit Brian Statham to the far corner of the ground and he and 'Nimble' set off running.

"S-e-v-e-r-a-l," shouted Bol.

"I'm with you," replied Nimble.

"Keep going, old boy, there's more yet," said Bol as they passed on the third run.

"I'm going as fast as I can," puffed Nimble.

They eventually ran five. This left Norman on strike and he was run out off the next ball attempting a sharp single. In fact he didn't get halfway down the wicket and had to be assisted from the pitch!

Trombones in the toilets

Cricket and rugby teams always fancy themselves as singers and at Lancashire we were no exception. We also did a very good impersonation of a brass band, under the leadership of Jack Bond. We would retire to the Gents and give a rendition of 'Abide With Me' or a selection of Glenn Miller's all-time greatest hits. We did not have any instruments. We just improvised to make the relevant noises of trumpet, saxophone, trombone, etc.

Late one evening in the Grand Hotel toilets at Leicester, we were in the middle of a particularly rousing selection of Sousa marches, when a pyjama-clad resident came down to reception complaining about the excessive noise that the band was making, and asking when, in fact, the dance would finish. He must have thought it was all a bad dream as the receptionist tried to explain that it was Lancashire County Cricket Club playing in the toilets!

   Why the toilets? The acoustics are better, of course. This also gave the group its 'professional' name – The Shithouse Serenaders.

Moonlight serenade

John Savage, the county coach, did actually play the trombone. After a particularly enjoyable evening when the Club were the guests of the Anglo-American Sporting Club at the Piccadilly Hotel in Manchester, 'Sav', Harry Pilling and I shared a taxi home. The conversation got round to the prowess of the Brighouse and Rastrick Brass Band which prompted Sav to say that he would give us a rendering of 'Little

Brown Jug' on his trombone when we arrived back at his house.

Sav went inside and re-appeared suitably armed with his trombone and proceeded to belt out a selection of his favourites. Harry and I applauded enthusiastically, but our enthusiasm was not shared by the residents of The Drive, Bury. This could have been loosely connected with the time, being 2.30 am. One bucket of water was thrown and one chap threatened to shove the trombone... Well, need I go any further.

Closing bars

The Glamorgan boys were the 'kings' of the singing – by tradition, I suppose. Eifion Jones, their wicket-keeper, invited our team to one of his benefit functions at Pontardulais Working Men's Club. Members of the world famous male voice choir would form part of the entertainment for the evening and Eifion, who had a beautiful voice, would also sing a solo.

It was a wonderful evening and a great experience to hear all those Welsh voices. Towards the end of the evening the Master of Ceremonies asked if any of the English, or Lancastrian members of the audience, to be precise, would care to 'give us a song'. Boyo, look you, Eistedfodd...we may have got the better of Glamorgan at cricket, but we knew our place as singers. We were very much Fourth Division compared to their Premier League performers. That is to say the Lancastrians in our party knew our place.

Our opening batsman, Barry Wood, was a Yorkshireman. *He* fancied himself as a Paul McCartney or, as they say on the Working Men's Club Circuit, Vocalist (Versatile). He said he would give them 'Hey Jude'. I can only conclude by saying that if any WMC (Affiliated) has difficulty clearing the club at 'time, gentlemen, please', they should call on the talents of B. Wood – Vocalist (Versatile). He will empty the place in two minutes flat. Flat being the operative word. He sounded like someone dragging a fender up a back street.

There's nothing like experience

Brian Close epitomised the British bulldog spirit. He was as hard as nails with that tremendous will to win.

Lancashire played Somerset at Southport in 1977. Lancashire won the game in two days largely because Colin Croft bowled a couple of really hostile spells, although Viv Richards scored 189 in the first innings. The game was over very quickly on the second day as Somerset were bowled out cheaply. Closey and I shook hands after the game and the

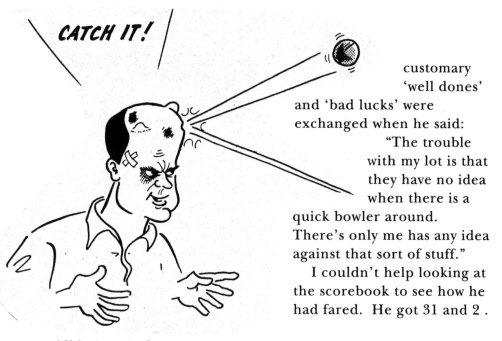

CATCH IT!

customary 'well dones' and 'bad lucks' were exchanged when he said:

"The trouble with my lot is that they have no idea when there is a quick bowler around. There's only me has any idea against that sort of stuff."

I couldn't help looking at the scorebook to see how he had fared. He got 31 and 2 .

All boys together

Brian Close was a great success at Somerset and the lads down there loved him. He used to call them all 'lad'. It was:

"Now then, Denis, lad or Ian, lad or Derek, lad," all the time.

They reckon that he once asked the tealady:

"Now then, Ethel lad, how about a cup of tea?"

Fielding practice

Closey was revered as a man who didn't know what pain was. His England colleagues say that he said:

"I will field at short leg when Derek Underwood is bowling to Clive Lloyd. When Lloyd sweeps the ball will hit me, and the other close-in fielders can catch the rebounds."

And he was serious.

CAREFREE CARIBBEANS

Whenever the West Indies are about to arrive on tour someone will always come out with:

"They're not as good as they were"

or

"They're not as strong as previous sides."

It is just wishful thinking.

Pure genius

The only cricketing fraternity not shaking in their shoes at the prospect of facing the West Indies are the Irish who have never been able to understand what all the fuss is about ever since Goodwin and O'Riordan worked the oracle at Sion Mills in 1969. Clive Lloyd's excuse was that 1969 was a particularly good year for the Guinness.

Give the lads a chance!

A peculiar quirk of a West Indies tour is the number of senior county batsmen who feel that it is perhaps better if some of the younger lads play against the West Indies to gain 'valuable experience'. This is, of course, for the good of the team. These are the same senior batsmen who insist that they play against New Zealand, India, Sri Lanka or Zimbabwe – 'to keep in touch'!

Beaches apart

Where do the West Indies keep finding their players? It is not just the quantity of players but the quality that is amazing. Suddenly a young lad appears who just happens to have a classic, economical action – at around 80 mph – another Ian Bishop.

Of course, the Caribbean is tailor-made for cricket with the game being the national pastime and almost a religion. Beach cricket certainly helps to develop the game and the players. The game is played right at the tide's edge where the sand is firm and moist and the ball really skids quickly off the surface. In England, of course, the tide is always either coming in or going out which means that you have to keep moving the pitch, and sea-fielders are in danger of being swept away.

West Indian beach games last for days, too. In England we get too many disturbances. Try walking along the beach in Barbados with a dozen kids sat on donkeys, or wandering about with headphones and a Geiger counter looking for buried treasure and the beach-cricketers will soon let you know what is what. Try burying grandad in the middle of the outfield and you will probably hear something like:

"Jeez, what de raas claat bumba-hole, man."

Which, roughly translated, means: "Can you go and bury grandad somewhere else, mate, we have got a game on here."

The Mindoo Philip Method
They love their cricket in the Caribbean and will go to great lengths to get a game started regardless of the setbacks.

On a recent trip to St Lucia with Lancashire County Cricket Club, I was 'wheeled' out of retirement for a game against the island side at the Mindoo Philip Ground. It rained on the evening prior to the game and popular chat from our players, sat around the Sip 'n' Dip bar, was that the game would be called off. Nobody seemed too bothered either.

When we arrived at the ground the following day it was, in fact, under water. Our lads felt, regrettably, that it would have to be back again to the Sip 'n' Dip for the rest of the day.

Mindoo Philip, a great St Lucian cricketer of his day, was the groundsman and he was determined that we would play. The 180 Lancashire members following the tour were also keen to see some action and they had positioned themselves in the covered stand square to the wicket. I could tell that Mindoo was head groundsman because he had the thick flip-flops on. He shouted to a chap with thin flip-flops, who I guessed to be one of the workers:

35

"Bring on de gas, man, bring on de gas."

The worker returned with a two gallon drum of petrol which was leaking. Mindoo instructed him to:

"T'row de gas, man, t'row de gas."

The chap proceeded to throw it everywhere – on the wicket, over the run-ups, over his flip-flops, his T-shirt, his shorts.

"Light de gas, man, light de gas," Mindoo said.

'I am off', I thought, and retired up-wind of the petrol. A match was thrown and they set fire to the wicket! There was smoke everywhere with flames leaping 20ft into the air. There was also much coughing and spluttering from our members as all the smoke drifted into the stands. Out in the middle we could hear things like:

"What the hell is going on, they must be barbecuing t' teams!"

When the flames died down, our friend swept all the debris away and, would you believe it, we started in half an hour. I have often wondered if Harry Brind, our Inspector of Pitches, and groundsman at The Oval, had thought of using the Mindoo Philip method of drying.

MINOR COUNTY EXCURSIONS

After retiring from Lancashire County Cricket Club I played Minor Counties cricket with Cumberland. I had a truly enjoyable time with a superb club and a great bunch of players.

Leave it to the captain

Our captain, John Moyes, had the patience of Job and put up with a lot of our mischievous pranks. All the usual things: nailing his cricket case to the floor, or filling it with house bricks, hoisting his underwear up the flag pole, and perhaps the best of the lot, picking up his Citroen CV6 and depositing it in the nearest field.

John was also captain at Workington Cricket Club, whose professional was Qasim Omar, the Pakistani Test batsman. Qasim, too, had a spell with Cumberland. We played a game at Netherfield Cricket Club, Kendal, and Qasim had brought his family along in the sponsored car provided for him by Workington. The car had a roof rack and written on the side was Qasim Omar, Workington and Pakistan. It didn't look the part somehow.

John told Qasim that if he wanted to take the family shopping around Kendal he, John, would drive the car to the ground for him. Qasim readily agreed. The Netherfield ground is beautiful, with a ruined castle high up as a back-drop. At the castle end of the ground there is a plateau for spectators to view the game and above this is another plateau where cars can be parked, it is also another great place from which to watch.

John parked the car on the top plateau, walked down onto the ground and went to inspect the wicket. Bernard Reidy, one of our players, and I, were attempting the *Telegraph* crossword. I looked up, momentarily, and couldn't believe what I saw.

"Isn't that Qasim's car on the move up there?" I said.

"Yes," said Bernard, "and there doesn't seem to be anyone sat in it."

We watched with great interest as the car gathered momentum. It bounced down onto the lower plateau with a heck of a bang before careering down the hillside and coming to rest crashed against the concrete benches surrounding the ground. The only parts of the car which seemed intact were the roof rack and the exhaust pipe. It was a complete write-off. John had obviously forgotten to engage the hand-brake. He was very distressed, but, of course, we all thought it was hilarious.

There was more to follow. Qasim eventually arrived at the ground, immediately spotted the wreck, and in that Pakistani style of English said:

"Captain, please, what is happening to my car?"

"I'm sorry, Qasim, there's been a slight accident," said John, "but don't worry. I am sure your insurance will cover it."

Qasim had a rather puzzled look on his face as he said: "Insurance, what is insurance?"

No more Mr Nice Guy

Our opening bowler at Cumberland, David Halliwell, or 'Mad Hally', as we called him, was an absolute riot on the field. A very quiet, meek and gentle man off the field, but once he had his cricket whites on it really was 'light the blue touch paper and stand clear'.

If a batsman were to get hold of him and hit him for a couple of fours or a six, he had been known to go completely off his trolley and shout down the wicket:

"That's it, pal, that's enough, no more Mr Nice Guy. They are all coming your way now. You're going to get the lot. Liquorice Allsorts, bumpers, beamers, 15-yarders, head-hunters – you name it, I can bowl it!"

The trouble was that far from intimidating the batsman they

used to crack up and just laugh at him.

One year, when we had qualified for the NatWest Trophy, we were drawn against Worcestershire at Worcester. We had a team meeting and Hally said:

"I can't wait to bowl at their big shots Hick and Botham. I'll reserve some of me specials for 'em."

We played the game and Hally actually bowled Graeme Hick. He promptly ran down the wicket, arm aloft with his finger raised.

"That's the one, you can't play them," he shouted to Hick.

The only problem was that Hick had scored 138.

BACK TO THE LEAGUE

I came back to Accrington CC as professional in 1984 after retiring from Lancashire. All the wickets tend to be a little damp in the League and I struggled to get many runs.

Not so finger-lickin' good
Part way through the season we had a drought and a stand-pipe ban was brought in. I thought, 'brilliant, they won't be able to water the wicket this week. There is a good chance that it will dry out into a flat batting track.' I drove into the ground and could see the wicket glistening in the sunlight. I said to Harry, the groundsman:

"The wicket looks a bit wet, Harry."
"Yes, there's 500 gallons gone on there this week," he said.
"You want to be careful with this stand-pipe ban in operation," I said. "You will be for the high jump if the

authorities find out."

"Oh, there's no problem," he said. "I've emptied the cesspit. I have only come across to tell you, if you pick the ball up today, don't lick your fingers!"

Battlefield at Bacup

We played at Bacup on one occasion and the wicket was that bad that as a batsman you didn't know whether to hit the ball or the sod of earth that came up with it. It was at the height of the Falklands War and our players thought that the Bacup wicket should have been twinned with Goose Green.

Billy, Bishop and a bouncer

At Accrington we got to the semi-final of the Cup competition and were drawn away against Todmorden Cricket Club who had Ravi Ratnayake, the Sri Lankan Test player, as professional. We were quite confident that we could win the game as Ratnayake had been having a mediocre season. We arrived at the ground and noticed that the Sri Lankan was nowhere to be seen.

We were having our knock up when this huge West Indian with a cricket case sauntered across the ground. All our lads were saying, "Who's that?" I knew who it was. None other than Ian Bishop, the West Indian opening bowler. Todmorden had hired him for the day from Derbyshire County Cricket Club as Ratnayake had been injured in a previous game and was unable to play. Not a bad swap if I might say so.

Bishop bowled very quickly but our openers battled it out and were 60 plus without loss. Then Todmorden got a break through and we lost wickets steadily. Our wicket-keeper, Billy Rawstron, was next man in. Billy had said in the dressing room that he didn't think that Bishop was very quick and that he would not be wearing a helmet. I thought at the time that that would be an unwise ploy on Billy's part. Billy had also said that he would be hooking if Bishop bowled him a bouncer. Again, I thought, not a very sensible thing to do.

Sure enough, Bishop unleashed a bouncer. It hit Billy full in the mouth, just as he was lifting his bat, and knocked him straight back onto the stumps. After a short while we brought Billy round and, as we were assisting him from the field, he stopped and protested:

"Hey, I can't be out like that, I had completed my shot."

"Billy, you hadn't even started your shot," I said. "Let's go and find a dentist."

As it was, Billy Rawstron went out and kept wicket with blood pouring from his mouth and flatly refused any treatment until after the game. They certainly breed 'em hard in the leagues.

Dog in the deep
Accrington has probably the best fielder in the world. I certainly have never seen one better. It is a Jack Russell terrier called Penny who has the proud distinction, along with its master, Sam, of not having lost any ball which has been hit out of the ground and into the thick undergrowth beyond, either in match or practice for 10 years. Other clubs have heard about Penny and contracts for her services have been received from as far afield as Derbyshire.

THE ART OF THE PROFESSIONAL SPECTATOR

League cricket has its own brand of humour and this usually revolves around the spectators.

The chief Barker

The Barker family, consisting of father, Keith and his two sons, Andrew and Garfield, played, until recently, for Enfield. In one particular game Enfield were out in the field when a dog ran onto the pitch. 'Big Roland', one of the local barrackers came out of the bar and shouted:

"Get that dog off t' pitch, there's enough Barkers out theer!"

The Rawtenstall Inquisitor

Jackie Barnes is the star of the Rossendale Valley barrackers and particularly of his home club, Rawtenstall. He just keeps asking questions, and if he gets you in a corner you are in for a real interrogation. He collared me on one occasion when Accrington, my home town club, were playing Rawtenstall.

"Who's playing?" he asked.

"Accrington," I replied, and then it went on.

"Who's their pro?"

"I am."

"What's your name?"

"Lloyd."

"Where do you live?"

"Accrington."

"How far is it?"

"About 3 miles."

"How do you get there?"

"Down the by-pass."

It went on and on and finished up with him asking me how Preston had got on against Wigan at football and what colour did they play in.

Any questions?
The Rawtenstall players tell a tale of the club's trip around the local Blackburn-based brewery. The coach set off from Rawtenstall and took the party to the brewery where they were met by an official who was to give them the formal tour which would end with complimentary drinks in the hospitality suite. Obviously, for the visitors, the business end of the trip was the last bit.

The party was taken through all the various stages of brewing by the official, whose comments went something like:

"This is where the hops and yeast are added to the special spring water which is supplied to the site by an artesian well. Here the beer is allowed to ferment and then finings are added to clear the brew and drop the sediment to the bottom of the tank.

"On to the next level, gentlemen, and we see the beer pumped into the kegs or bottles which are then appropriately stamped and labelled.

"Down to the next level and the bottles are crated up and stacked automatically before finally arriving at the ground floor, ready for collection and distribution by our own dray wagon fleet.

"Now, before we adjourn for a drink, are there any questions?"

Need he have asked? Jackie Barnes is off again:

"When is it Blackburn holidays?"

Keep 'em guessing

Accrington CC has its own barracker who goes by the name of 'Barbs'. He turns up at every game in jeans, T-shirt and a top hat. He shouts the same thing every time the ball is fielded:

"Well done, that man. Yeah – give us a thumb!"

I think it must be some sort of coded message.

Points of reference

The language in the middle can also a bit different in league cricket. After all the years of county cricket and third man, fine leg, cover point and square leg, etc. it was quite a shock to turn up at Rishton and hear their captain, Eric Whalley, setting the field. He would say:

"Robbie, round a bit to that wastepaper bin; Mick, next to that woman in t' red dress; Wellsy, by that bloke with the dog."

I used to stand at the crease with my head on a swivel thinking, 'where the heck is he putting them?'

Classic comments

One of the best barrackers I heard was Old Trafford's Norman Williams, or Norman the Postman, as we knew him. He had all the usual sayings. When an opposition batsman was stepping onto the pitch, Norman would say:

"Don't close the gate, you won't be long"

or

"Hey, mate, there is a 'phone call for you. I've told 'em to hang on, you won't be a minute"

or
"Bowl him a piano, see if he can play that"
or
"You'll never die of a stroke, pal."

He used to really have a go at Derbyshire's
opening batsman, Alan Hill, who had a great
defence and could certainly hang around. In
one game Alan was blocking out and the
scoreboard wasn't moving at all. After an hour
and a half he was 4 not out. The afternoon
papers had just come out and Norman was sat
reading. He looked up and shouted:
  "Hey, Hill. You're 3 not out in the Stop
Press, see if you can get to 6 before the Final
Edition."

YOU'RE NOT IN THE
OBITUARY COLUMN,
SO YOU MUST STILL
BE ALIVE...!

The trains go past Old Trafford at 20 minute intervals and during another game three trains went by as Alan Hill amassed 2 runs. Norman had noticed this and shouted:

"Hey, Hill, the trains are winning 3-2."

Going down with the team

Draught Bass Harry, who used to attend Lancashire matches in the early Sixties was better known for his deeds rather than his words. The story goes that he used to have a pint of draught Bass every time a Lancashire wicket fell. At that time the county did not have a particularly strong batting line-up and invariably took lunch with the score something like 70 for 8. They had to ban Harry from the ground because he was incoherent by 1 o'clock.

HELLO, LOOKS AS IF LANCASHIRE HAVE COLLAPSED AGAIN....

STEPHENSON'S STOUT

EY UP...

LASTING MEMORIES

Captain of England?

I had an outside chance of captaining England at one stage of my career. I was brought back for the one-day Internationals against the West Indies in 1980. I was told I would be batting at Number 7 and if I showed up well, got a few runs, and handled the quicks OK, I would be in the swim of things, with a couple of others, when it came to the captaincy. I remember taking guard and watching Malcolm Marshall walking back to his bowling mark before his run up. I thought to myself, 'Where is he going? I don't go that far for my holidays!'

He set off towards me. I think he had reached the sawdust when again I thought, 'I don't think he wants me to play forward to this delivery'. There was an almighty flurry of arms and legs as he reached the crease and unleashed this 90 mph thunderbolt at me. I played what can only be described in any MCC coaching manual as a very hurried backward defensive prod. The ball smashed into my forearm and broke it in two places. I distinctly remember thinking, as I was assisted from the field, 'I wonder if I have done enough?'

Best knock I ever played

I remember one particular game in Water Street, Accrington, where I was brought up. The game was England versus Pakistan because one of my pals was a Pakistani lad from the next street. I suppose my Water Street background did have an influence on my overall game at Old Trafford.

People used to say that I was quick between the wickets. Well you had to

be quick off the mark in
Water Street, particularly if
you wanted first use of the
outside, long drop, tippler
toilet which three other families
used to share. If you did manage
to get in first you would whistle and
put your foot up against the handle
to make sure you didn't have unwanted
guests. It didn't help too much in Water
Street because the door opened outwards and
everybody used to pile in anyway. In those days, too, I
remember that there was no 'Andrex' or 'Delsey', it was the
Daily Sketch or *Daily Herald* cut up into little squares and nailed
onto the back of the door that had to suffice.

Anyway, back to the match. England won the toss and
elected to bat – the cobbles were wet and I thought it would be
a bit tricky when they dried. You always pretended to be one of
the top players of the day, Cowdrey, May, Graveney. This
particular day, I was Colin Cowdrey. England had reached 520-
3 with 'Cowdrey' 320 not out. My little Pakistani friend was
always Hanif Mohammad and his figures were 0-470.

People often ask at cricket forums, "What was the best knock
you ever played?" Well, that was it. I was in for 23 weeks.
'Hanif' could not get me out, and when it was his turn to bat, it
was pouring with rain and he didn't get a knock!

If the name fits

I was once out in a University game and the scorebook read –
D. LLOYD caught KINKEAD-WEEKES bowled WINGFIELD-
DIGBY 0. Our scorer came into the dressing room and said:

"Thank goodness you were not DAVID EDMUND
ALGERNON FORTESCUE-LLOYD, we would never have got it
on the scorecard."

Spotting the weakness

I played for Lancashire against South Africa at Old Trafford in 1965. Brian Statham brought me on to bowl the last over before lunch to their tall left-handed batsman. I had watched him play during the morning and felt that he might be vulnerable around leg stump. I attacked him in that area and finished up with the figures 1-0-0-24. He hit every ball either over, past, through or wide of square leg. I walked off with our senior players and asked,

"Who's that?"

One replied, "He's called Graeme Pollock. He will never make a good player. Too free."

The invisible call and a silent appeal

I was invited to captain the MCC against Oxford University at The Parks and eagerly accepted. It was an opportunity to get out my old MCC touring sweaters and open the batting against 'the boys'. As I was skipper, I made out the batting order. Of course I would be opening, and I paired myself with Bob Lanchbury, who had a spell with Worcestershire, but, more recently, was a prolific run-scorer for Old Hill in the Birmingham League. Bob was also deaf. Before we went out to the middle he said to me:

"When you call you must always look at me so I can lip read your call. But make sure you look at me."

Everything was plain sailing for a while. I had managed a few singles and was seeing the ball well. If I carried on as I was I would surely score the hundred I had set out my stall for. I played a cut to square cover where the left-handed fielder had

to move a good five metres to his right. An easy single, I thought, and called "Yes". I forgot to look at Bob and set off up the track. I was halfway down the wicket when I had that moment of panic and thought to myself, 'Where is he, I should have passed him by now?'

I looked up and Bob was leaning on his bat and mouthing, "No!" I about-turned and bolted back to my end. The ball was on its way back to the keeper. I made a full length despairing dive in my MCC regalia and still finished 1 yard short. I was covered from top to toe in mud, grass clippings and sawdust.

Bob didn't care for fielding and said that he had some work to do in the City but would be back for the second innings. I said:

"I am going to keep you and I well apart in the second innings, Bob. You can open and I will bat Number 11."

This suited Bob because I don't think he had batted any lower than two in his life. Out he went again with a new partner. In the first over there was a tremendous appeal for a caught behind from the Oxford team which I am sure you could have heard in Cambridge. Bob stood his ground but the umpire duly gave him out. When he got back to the pavilion he was asked if he had got a touch, seeing that he hadn't walked.

"Oh, yes," he said, "I definitely hit it but I didn't think anyone had appealed."

David Lloyd – long-distance runner
Lancashire versus Warwickshire at Southport in 1982 was an extraordinary game of cricket and well worth recalling. Gladstone Small had been called up to join the England squad but was later released to rejoin the Warwickshire team. In the meantime, David Brown, the Warwickshire manager, was given permission by the TCCB to take Small's position in the team and to bowl in his place. Brown in fact bowled 13 overs in the first innings and took one wicket. Small later bowled 15 overs in the same innings and also took a wicket. Warwickshire had

effectively played 12 players, although it didn't seem to bother the Lancashire team as we rattled up 414 for 6 declared. This was in reply to the Warwickshire first innings total of 523 for 4 declared, in which Geoff Humpage, the wicket-keeper, had scored 254 and Alvin Kallicharran, the former West Indies batsman and captain, had been undefeated on 230.

Robin Dyer, he of many names (R.I.H.B. Dyer on the scorecard), bagged a pair, while Graeme Fowler, the Lancashire opener, scored two centuries in the game and hardly ran a run. He pulled a muscle early in his first innings and had a runner (me) for the remainder of that innings and for the whole of his second innings.

Warwickshire were bowled out for 111 on the third morning of the game by Leslie Leopold McFarlane, a West Indian, qualified for England, who had joined us from Northants. I remember it was a beautiful morning with not a cloud in the sky, but, incredibly, the ball swung 'sideways' as they say. We were left to score 226 to win the game and did so by 10 wickets. I was Graeme Fowler's opening partner and I didn't fancy getting out and having to run all his runs for him again, so I decided to get a few for myself.

Never fully appreciated
When I played the game I never felt that I really got the credit that I deserved. When I go to speak at dinners, the chairman

for the evening will, more often than not, give me the big build up. So many thousand runs, so many hundreds, etc, etc. They always omit to say I scored none in my first innings for Lancashire and being a consistent sort of player, scored none in the second innings. Furthermore, it took more than one hour and a half at the crease to register the dreaded 'pair'. I seemed to become typecast by the press after that. When I did manage to score a few I invariably got the following reviews in the press.

'It was a painstaking knock by Lloyd ... always ill at ease ... never in command ...'

I always used to read the papers and sometimes used to think, 'That's a bit unfair. I didn't think I did too badly today.' Of course when I retired in 1983 things died down. I suppose, out of sight out of mind.

David Hughes, the Lancashire captain, has a long memory and, after Graham Lloyd had scored 100 in 80 balls against Kent, was heard to remark:

"Well, watching that it is obvious that your father has had no input, whatsoever, into your game."

In simple black and white
When I signed for Cumberland, I did a local radio interview by telephone. We chatted for a while about the team's prospects and my role in the team. The chap finished up by asking me:

"Do you think you will adapt to the Cumberland weather after spending so much time in the West Indies?"

I was a little confused and replied:

"I have never been to the West Indies, I'm David Lloyd, not Clive."

I heard the interviewer shout to his colleagues:

"Hey, they've signed the wrong one!"

You wouldn't believe that Clive and I could ever get mistaken for each other, but we did. On reflection I can understand why. We were both left-handed for a start, and we both played in that same debonair fashion which put the fear of God up every opposition bowler...well, one of us did anyway. On one occasion we were walking out to bat together after being not out on the previous evening when we heard two members talking on the Old Trafford steps.

"Are the two Lloyds brothers?" one asked.

"I don't think so," replied the other, "but I think one of them wears spectacles."

There is another distinguishing feature. I have seen Clive in the showers, but that is another story.

Lancashire Lloyds – the next generation

The whole thing reared its head again in 1989 when my son scored his maiden century for Lancashire. I thought 'I'm bound to get a mention here in the press. They are bound to see the name and put two and two together. They are bound to know who he is.'

IF THEY ARE BROTHERS, THE ONE OBVIOUSLY SPENDS MUCH LONGER AT THE WICKET THAN THE OTHER...

The press probably did put two and two together but on this occasion it made five. The same paragraph appeared in nearly all the Lancashire cricket reports. It said, 'Graham Lloyd, son of legendary West Indian captain Clive .....'

Even Clive got the backlash because he had people ringing

from the West Indies to congratulate him on his son's
achievement, which was no mean feat because his lad, Jason,
was only eight at the time!

Great Characters

JACK SIMMONS

Jack Simmons joined Lancashire very late in life for a professional cricketer. He came into county cricket at the age of 29 after playing for a host of clubs around the Lancashire leagues. During his time at Lancashire he developed into a genuine character and never really lost his amateur ways, which at times turned out to be quite hilarious.

The punter's priorities

In Jack's first 'Roses' match we batted first and had a particularly good morning session, scoring well over a hundred runs without losing a wicket. This was particularly satisfying for us as we had been on the receiving end in recent games against Yorkshire. Our captain, Jack, Bond, wanted to keep the momentum going and to continue the good work. He called all the troops into the dressing room after lunch to fire us up for the afternoon session, but only ten turned up. 'Simmo' was nowhere to be seen.

They searched all the usual places, toilet, snack bar, physio's room. He was nowhere. Eventually our scorer, 'Mac' Taylor tracked him down in the closed circuit TV monitor room, headphones on, racing paper open, listening to the 1.45 from Wetherby. Mac said that he thought Jack ought to report back to the dressing room as the captain had just got all the lads together for a little meeting.

"Tell 'im I won't be long, I'm just listening to this race, I've got a tenner on t' favourite."

Mac told him that that was perhaps not the answer the captain would want to hear at this time of the proceedings, especially against Yorkshire!

Creative training

Jack was never too thrilled with pre-season training. The diet was *always* starting tomorrow, the leg always played up a bit which prevented any running. Oh, and he was *thinking* about packing up smoking.

We used to finish our morning sessions with a three to five mile run around Chorlton and Old Trafford. Simmo knew every short cut there was. He was spotted in various places which bore no resemblance to the route we were supposed to take. He was seen alighting from an articulated wagon at the gates of Old Trafford, having flagged the driver down and told him he was lost. He was also seen slumped in the doorway of the Throstle's Nest pub suffering from an acute stitch.

On another occasion he set off on the run with the *Manchester Evening News* under his arm. The reason for that was that he had seen one or two houses for sale in the area which he thought he might buy and change into flats, then rent them out to our players who lived well away from Old Trafford, or to trialists and visiting spectators!

High finance

Jack's locker was like a miniature office. One day there were papers, bills and invoices strewn about all over the place. Steven O'Shaughnessy asked if he had lost something.

"Aye," said Jack, "I've put thirty grand in an account

somewhere and can't find it anywhere. Anyway, somebody will send me in a statement and then I'll know where it is."

Steven was perhaps the last person to say this to as he had just come off the telephone after trying to persuade the bank manager to advance him £200 to buy a car. He went out of the room scratching his head and muttering:

"He must be playing a different game to me."

Sitting pretty

The lads would always be looking to take a rise out of Jack, Graeme Fowler in particular. In one match at Old Trafford Jack had batted particularly well, and had practically won the game single-handed. He got a terrific ovation from the crowd and all the lads mobbed him when he got back upstairs.

'Foxy' Fowler told Jack that the lads had decided to make a presentation to him in view of him playing so well. It was something that Jack would find extremely useful, he went on to say. Jack eagerly took off the wrapping and the brown paper and there it was, the ideal present for Simmo. It was a toilet seat with the following items strapped to it – a packet of fags, a box of matches, a telephone, *The Sporting Life* and a can of lager!

A small starter

Jack's appetite is legendary and not without good reason. After all, he has had one delicacy in a local chip shop named after him on the menu. It is the imaginatively named the 'Jack Simmons Special' consisting of pudding, chips and peas with a fish on top. It is known as *nouvelle cuisine* in Great Harwood where Jack lives.

On returning home from an away fixture late one night Jack asked me to drop him off at his favourite chippy. He ordered one of his famed specials and then sat on the wall outside and proceeded to demolish the lot. I did happen to enquire:

"Why don't you take them home and eat them there, Simmo?"

"No," he said, "if I did that Jacqueline wouldn't make my any supper."

Challenge accepted

Once, during a game at Blackpool, he booked a table for four at Morton Fisheries, which is a sit-in chippy about a mile from the ground. So what, you may ask. What's so special about that? Well, he booked it during the lunch interval!

Lancashire were fielding and Jack led the charge off the field. He and his fellow diners, Clive Lloyd included, drove off to the chippy in their cricket gear and got stuck in. Jack had the 'usual', pudding, chips and peas with a fish on top. Apparently it was hilarious. The customers couldn't believe that part of the team were away from the ground and dining in style, so to speak. One chap watched Jack demolish his plateful and, with a smile on his face, said

"If you can eat that lot again I will pay for it."

What a challenge for our hero. He set to again and polished off another special. On the way back I think it was Clive who said:

"Simmo, you must be full to bursting."

"I am" replied Jack, "but I wanted him to pay up. I know him, he's a tight bastard!"

A proper lunch

There was another occasion at Liverpool. Lancashire were in the field and Jack was giving frantic signs to the dressing room from his position at second slip. What was required? Was it tactics, a shrewd field change, another sweater or maybe a stud had come loose? John Abrahams, our resident 12th man at the time ran out, spoke to Jack and came back doubled up with laughter.

"You'll never guess what he wants," he said. "He wants a pencil and paper so that he can go round the fielders, umpires

and batsmen to take a lunch order for fish and chips because it is always a salad at Liverpool. He says only rabbits can live off that stuff!"

The painful truth
In a game at Trent Bridge, I think it was during Clive Lloyd's reign as captain, we had Jack fielding at widish mid-off which meant he would have quite a long chase if the ball was driven back past him. Sure enough a well struck half-volley was despatched just beyond Simmo's reach. Our hero tramped off after it and caught be ball up just inside the boundary rope. At this stage the batsmen had run a leisurely three. As Jack stopped the ball a wag in the crowd shouted,

"Come on, Simmo, you big fat bastard."

At this Clive bellows after him, "Hey man, what are you doin' down there?"

"He's just called me a big fat bastard," shouts our offended mid-off.

"Well you are a big fat bastard," says Clive. "Just throw the ball back, they've run five already."

Jousting with Javed
A similar situation arose in a game versus Glamorgan only this time it was not a spectator who offended Simmo. This time it was one of the opposition players. It was none other than Javed Miandad, who, it is strongly rumoured, is as popular as acne on the playing circuit.

Jack was bowling a good, tight economical spell and had tied Javed down for the first five balls of an over. Javed pushed the next ball towards the off side and threatened to run. Jack was onto it as quick as a flash, and stood with the ball between his feet. Most players would have retreated back into the crease but Javed stood his ground about five yards down the track. The umpire, quite rightly, didn't call over as he anticipated further developments to the sixth ball of Jack's over.

He wasn't disappointed.

"Come on, fat Jack, throw the ball," goaded Miandad.

Now Jack was affectionately known throughout the cricketing world as 'Flat Jack' because he bowled his off-spinners quick, with a flat trajectory. I am sure that Javed knew this but deliberately called him *fat* Jack. The 'proverbial' hit the fan in a big way.

"Who are you calling fat Jack, you sawn off little bastard, get back in that crease."

Javed didn't. He kept inching forward and Jack bent lower towards the ball. All of a sudden Simmo swooped and hurled the ball at the stumps. Unfortunately, he missed and more unfortunately, Graeme Fowler, our wicket-keeper, also missed. In fact, he wasn't even there. Peter Lee, who was bowling at the other end and fielding in the deep square leg area, which was the general direction of where the ball was heading after Simmo had thrown it, didn't see it either. As it was the last ball of the over, he was moving towards his run-up and taking his sweater off at the same time. The ball careered over the boundary rope and into the advertising boards. The umpire duly signalled four and called the end of the over. Again Clive Lloyd was the captain.

"What's goin' on here man, what are you trying to do?" he shouted.

"I'm trying to run the bastard out," replied Jack in a rather threatening way.

Foxy Fowler couldn't stay out of this for long and came in with:

"I think he is trying to get you riled, Simmo."

"Yes, and he has bloody well succeeded," said

Simmo as he proceeded to kick his cap all the way to second slip.

Open verdict

It was well known that, during an Australia versus Pakistan Test

match, Dennis Lillee was seen and photographed kicking Javed Miandad straight up the backside. Many influential people in the game felt that this was certainly 'not cricket', that an example should have been made of Lillee and that he should have been severely disciplined.

Others thought that he hadn't kicked him hard enough....

One good turn deserves another

Simmo was also the king of the complimentary tickets. We were only allowed two per game but Jack used to conjure them up from all over the place. He didn't have the heart to tell people "No, I can't get you any", but he expected the same treatment when he wanted tickets for himself.

We had been rained off during a day at Chesterfield against Derbyshire. Simmo had seen in the local paper that The Tremeloes were appearing in cabaret at the local 'Palais'. He rounded up the lads, ordered the taxis and took us down to the 'gig'. There was a fair crowd gathering with quite a long queue. Jack marched up to the pay kiosk and informed the young lady that Lancashire County Cricket Club had arrived. The rather bemused girl said:

"Would you like to join the queue" and "It will be £1 each."

"No, you don't understand," said Jack. "It's Lancashire County Cricket Club. That's Clive Lloyd over there with Barry Wood, Frank Hayes, and the rest of the team."

"I'm sure it is, sir, but would you mind joining the queue –

it's £1 each," she repeated.

"No, no listen,' said Jack, "when your lads come up to Manchester they get 'comps' to get in places and it should be the same for us down here. We should get in for nowt."

The young lady had had enough by this time and came back with:

"I'm sure you should, but this is one place where it is a £1 each to get in."

"Right," said Simmo, leaning into the kiosk, "wait till you want some Gillette Cup tickets. Don't come to me for 'em!"

Some joined the queue, some went back, but it all left a rather bemused young lady wondering what on earth the Gillette Cup was.

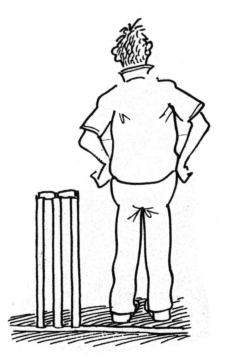

LADS FROM LANCASHIRE

Stan Worthington

In the late Fifties and early Sixties Lancashire had a coach called Stan Worthington. The senior players at that time Tommy Greenhough, Jack Dyson, Peter Marner and some of the younger uncapped players, like Harry Pilling and John Sullivan, used to tell great stories about Stan.

Apparently he used to dress immaculately and would invariably wear a cravat. He was also a stickler for manners and etiquette at the dinner table, and would always be at pains to educate 'the boys' as to which knife and fork to use and how to stir their tea, etc.

On one occasion a young trialist fast bowler sat opposite Stan for lunch. Mixed grill was on the menu, which included a full tomato. The youngster thrust his fork into the tomato and stuffed the whole thing into his mouth. It was absolutely piping hot and he immediately spat it out with such force that it landed in the middle of Stan's forehead – and stuck there! The older players said that even if the lad was quicker than Fred Trueman and Brian Statham combined he would never have opened the bowling for the county after that episode.

Stan used to rule with a rod of iron and the players were genuinely frightened of him. As usual in a dressing room, the players would try to play pranks on the coach but woe betide anyone that Stan found playing tricks on him.

One story goes that after a particularly enjoyable night in Newcastle, during a 2nd XI fixture against Northumberland, the boys noticed that Stan's trilby was hung up on the stand in the hotel lobby. They decided to play rugby with it. One of them stood with arms raised depicting 'the goals' whilst

another laid on the floor
holding the hat as they used to do
for conversions. The rest of them then took turns at kicking it
over the goal posts. When they had finished it looked rather
less like a trilby. The next morning was a very quiet affair until
Stan said in very measured tones:

"It has come to my notice that certain individuals found
great delight in kicking my hat, rugby fashion, around the
hotel. You will all have the same opportunity again this evening
but this time, gentlemen, my head will be underneath it!"

Colin Hilton

Also around at that time was Colin Hilton, a fast bowler from
the Leigh area of Lancashire. Colin was a great storyteller with
many tales about coal miners. He used to tell of the dreaded
condition which afflicted the majority of colliers known as clog
lock.

"What was clog lock?" we used to ask. Was it a breathing
condition or an infection of some kind.

Colin would explain, "No lad, nowt like that. It gets 'ot
down theer and so t' miners strip off down to their helmets and
clogs. When they get in a narrow seam they have to bend down
reight low and sometimes their left bollock gets trapped
between their ankle and their clog. That's clog lock – they
carry 'em out screaming wi' it."

Colin took the field at Lord's after a particularly heavy night
sampling the local London brews. He bounced through the
Long Room and was passing the members seated either side of
the gangway when he said:

"I feel like a bag o' shit this mornin'," and promptly spat out
the most foul looking 'green Gilbert' imaginable which landed
straight on a member's toe.

The member was last seen trying to remove the offending
'Gilbert' with his walking stick but with little success.

Barry Wood

My opening partner at Lancashire for a good number of years
was Barry Wood, and I used to room with him on away trips.
When we turned in for the night he would say his prayers, knelt
by the side of the bed. I was surprised to hear him finished one
night with:

"...and please, Lord, I hope I get 100 tomorrow."

He then got into his bed and I started thinking, 'I wonder
how many I am going to get tomorrow,' because usually one of
the openers goes cheaply. I was
about to ask him when he was
back by the side of the bed again.
He continued:

"I'm sorry, Lord, I forgot to say
100 not out."

YOU WERE A BIT
OFF FORM TODAY,
LORD...

Woody was a very brave batsman and superb hooker. When Andy Roberts arrived on the scene at Hampshire and was terrorising opening batsmen around the country, Woody was heard to say in our dressing room:

"I can't wait to get to Southampton and take that Roberts on. That will sort out the men from the boys. I am going to wind him up and tell him that he throws. He can bowl bouncers at me all day. He will never get me out."

The Southampton game came and the moment of truth arrived. Andy bowled the first ball to Woody with three sweaters on. It was just a gentle loosener. Woody patted it back down the pitch and as Andy was picking it up he said to him:

"Did you throw that, you big ...?"

Andy's eyes nearly popped out of his head. He immediately removed the three sweaters and added another five paces to his run-up. All our players were clamouring for a grandstand view, peering from the pavilion windows. Andy came steaming in and Woody was there, quickly into position to play the hook shot, only it wasn't a bouncer. It was a bail high full toss which demolished the top of middle stump. Our dressing room erupted. I don't know who was happier, us or the opposition.

Mick Malone

Mick Malone, the Australian swing bowler, was Lancashire's overseas player in 1980 and what an impression he made. He was quite the best practical joker I have ever come across. He had no sooner met all the players in the dressing room when he started paving the way for his party piece. He told us that most of his belongings had arrived except for his pet snake which had been in quarantine and would be available for collection in around a month's time. This put everyone on their guard and was the topic of conversation in the weeks leading up to the snake coming out of quarantine.

The date duly arrived and we had our first sighting of the reptile. Bob Ratcliffe, a medium-pace bowler from Accrington and now cricket master at Marlborough School, was a very nervy sort and had been more on edge than most at the prospect of encountering the snake.

Sure enough, he was the one who Mick picked on. He 'borrowed' Bob's spare locker key and put the snake into his locker in such a way that it would fall out as soon as the door was opened. Bob duly came in, opened his locker, and out popped the snake, straight at him. He was absolutely petrified, ran into the washrooms and locked himself in the toilet. Of course it was a rubber snake, but absolutely lifelike in every respect – colouring, feel and it actually wriggled as well.

IT WASN'T A BIRD-EATING SNAKE...!

'Dickie' Bird, the Test Match umpire, didn't escape either. After all, Dickie is a prime target and another nervy character. Mick got at Dickie during the lunch interval in a game he was standing in at Old Trafford. Mick primed the waitress to serve Dickie a special lunch on one of those silver serving dishes with a domed cover. The waitress went to Dickie's table with the serving dish and said to Dickie that the chef had cooked him a special lunch.

"Ee, thanks very much, luv," said Dickie picking up his knife and fork.

The dome came off and there was the snake. Dickie literally

flew out of the dining room, down the pavilion steps, across the outfield to the middle of the square and flatly refused to come back into the pavilion.

Perhaps the best prank Mick ever pulled with the snake was on the club members. A number of hard drinkers used to congregate under the pavilion clock at Old Trafford and as the day went on and more beer was consumed, the louder they got. As players we used to think that they were good fun but the opposition and the umpires didn't think so because they were often the butt of their barracking.

One day Mick meticulously tied nylon thread onto the tail end of the snake, and at around 4 o'clock in the afternoon, when the beer had taken hold and the members were in full flow, he went to work. He went onto the players' balcony and very carefully lowered the snake towards where the members were congregated. He lined it up just above the eye-level of one particular chap and directly in line with the pint pot which he was holding. He then swiftly dunked the snake in the pint pot and equally quickly whipped it back onto the balcony. The poor chap shouted, "B..... Hell!" and promptly dropped his pint onto the floor, smashing it to bits.

"What's up wi' you, Bert?" asked his mate. "Can't you stand the pace?"

By this time everyone around was looking to see what had caused the commotion.

"Did you see that?" asked Bert. "A snake just dropped into my pint."

The whole place erupted.

"A snake, a snake!" chuckled his mate. "Go and get me a pint of what you have just had, it might get me next!"

And it did.

Steven O'Shaughnessy

Steven O'Shaughnessy was a very talented cricketer who played

at Lancashire before moving to Worcestershire. He should
have gone much further in the game than he did but maybe
that was the way he wanted it. He certainly kept the dressing
room amused though, and it seemed that every time he opened
his mouth, he put his foot in it. He would get really tongue-
tied and things would not come out as they should have.

There was a dressing-room vote on an issue relating to pay
and Steven was asked his opinion.

"I'll go arrest with the long of them," he said.

Another time he was in a discussion about a very good
looking film star and he said,

"I bet he can pull the birds. I expect he'll have five
girlfriends at a time, three on each arm."

And then there was,

"She's smart, over there," he said.

"Which one?" asked his mate.

"That blonde with the dark hair," he said.

Perhaps the best 'Shauny' story was when he was asked to be
night-watchman in a game at Old Trafford. Graeme Fowler and
I opened the batting and had that uncomfortable half-hour
to negotiate before close of play. Fortunately, we did not
lose a wicket that evening, but Graeme was out very early the
next morning. When I was out in the middle I always used
to look up at our balcony to see who was coming in next and
I saw Clive Lloyd rise, put his gloves on, and pick up his
bat.

I did a little gardening on the wicket and then looked
towards the pavilion. It was not Clive that appeared
down the pavilion steps but Shauny. He had got about
20 yards onto the pitch when there was a general buzz
from the members' pavilion, and Clive followed
down the steps and onto the field. I thought, 'Are
there any more coming out? Is this a sponsored
walk?'

Now, the Laws of the game state that once the incoming batsman is on the pitch, he is in and so Clive had to about turn and go back into the pavilion. I could see much arm waving and gesticulating through the pavilion window as I went across to have a word with Shauny.

"All right, Bumble, how is it going?" he asked.

"Fine for me, Steven, maybe not so fine for you. Why have you come in? Clive was on his way down the steps behind you," I said.

"No," he said, "he told me I was number three last night."

"You were night-watchman last night. This morning you go back to number eight." I explained.

"Well, that's not right. If I was number three last night, I should be number three this morning," he protested.

"I don't somehow think that Clive will see it like that," I replied.

"What should I do then, give my wicket away and let him come in?" he asked.

"No, just get stuck in and let's see what we can do because, looking up at that window, I think the longer you stay out here, the better it will be for your health," I said.

How did he play? Beautifully – he got 60 odd in even time.

Mike Watkinson

Mike Watkinson was interviewed on local radio after Lancashire had won the NatWest Trophy to go with the Benson and Hedges Cup in 1990.

He was asked if he thought Lancashire had come home with the bacon. He answered:

"Come home with the bacon? We've got the whole pig, mate!"

David Hughes

April is a good time for assessing the prospects for the coming season. Chris Tavaré, captain of Somerset, and David Hughes, captain of Lancashire, were asked at the start of the 1991 season what were their ambitions for the coming campaign.

Tavaré said:

"Quite simple, that Somerset do not finish bottom of the County Championship table."

David Hughes said:

"Well, we are a big county with great traditions. I cannot see anyone beating us in the Championship, we will go all the way in the NatWest and the Benson and Hedges, and we will definitely win the Refuge League and their Cup as well. On as personal note, I would like to score a thousand runs, take a hundred wickets, captain England to a 5-0 whitewash against the West Indies, be elected skipper for the World Cup in Australia and New Zealand and bring back the trophy for the country."

The interviewer paused before saying:

"You are taking the mickey, aren't you?"

Hughes replied, "Well, Tavaré started it!"

FAROKH ENGINEER

Lancashire, over the years, have had lots of local players with good old-fashioned names. John Tommy Tyldesley, Dick Tyldesley, Ernie Tyldesley, Harry Makepeace, Cyril Washbrook, Eddie Paynter, Ken Shuttleworth and many more. It is good to see that the present side is carrying the same traditional Lancashire names, Wasim Akram, Gehan Mendis and, of course, only a few years ago, Farokh Engineer, one of the best signings Lancashire County Cricket Club ever made. A brilliant wicket-keeper, flamboyant, unorthodox and aggressive batsman, brilliant team man and what a character.

OH AYE, AND WOULD THAT BE THE ACCRINGTON AKRAMS?

Following instructions
When he first joined us he lived on the south side of Manchester and could just about find his way to the ground at Old Trafford. It was a different story when we travelled to away games. The only road he seemed to know was the M6. That is fine

as most of the counties are in that general direction. The problem came when we were due to play Yorkshire at Headingley.

"M6?" asked Farokh.

"Yes, that's right," said Ken Snellgrove, our Scouse batsman, "just keep going, you can't miss it."

I don't know where he got to but four hours to Leeds from Manchester is a little over the top.

Comedians used to tell a joke about him, about the time when his car was in for service and he had to catch a bus back home to Sale.

The story goes that he asked his team-mates:

"How do I know which bus to get on?"

"It will tell you on the front of the bus, just ask for what it says on the bus," he was told.

The bus came along, Farokh got on it and asked for:

"One to Leyland Motors."

The driver said, "We don't go to Leyland Motors, pal. This is the Altrincham run."

"It says Leyland Motors on the front of the bus," said Farokh.

The driver replied, "Aye, and it says India on the tyres but we're not taking you home!"

Almost...is near enough!
Of course, when you sign a player of Farokh Engineer's calibre you know you have got a class performer. What you don't

know about the individual is what his thoughts are on gamesmanship and the darker side of the game. Farokh was a lovable rogue and we quickly found out what made him tick.

We were playing Kent at Old Trafford, Farokh was behind the sticks and I was at fine leg slip only about three yards from him. Incidentally, I should have worn glasses by this time but I didn't want the committee to know that I couldn't see too well. They might not have given me a new contract! Anyway, Frank Hayes was at first slip, and that highly-tuned, trained-to-perfection athlete, Jack Simmons, was at second slip. I think he was eating a pie at the time. Barry Wood was diagonally opposite me at gully. Peter Lever was bowling and Stuart Leary was the batsman.

Lever bowled a beauty which just took the edge of Leary's bat. Farokh dived away to his right and the ball smacked into his glove. Up he went for the catch in a big way but there was more of a stifled appeal from the rest. Leary turned round and he must have thought it was out because he walked off without looking at the umpire. 'What a great effort', I thought. But I'm sure it bounced.

I went across to Barry Wood and said, "He took that well, didn't he?"

"Oh, great effort," said Woody, "didn't he make a lot of ground?"

"It's funny," I said, "but from my angle it looked as if it might have bounced first."

"I didn't want to say anything," said Woody, "but I'm looking at it front on and I am sure it bounced."

"Well, let's go and have a word with Simmo, he looks as if he has finished his pie, let's see what he thinks."

"Great catch, Jack, eh?" I said.

"Brilliant," said Jack, "didn't he make a lot of ground, what a dive."

"It's funny," said Woody, "but the two of us thought that it might have bounced first."

"I wasn't going to say much," said Jack, "but he took it right in front of me and it definitely did bounce."

"Let's go and have a word with him, then," I said.

Now Farokh was no different to all the other Indian cricketers, in that when they are happy their heads start nodding, and his was going ten to the dozen.

"Great catch, Rooky, brilliant effort. It all happened so quick but the three senior players thought that there might have been the semblance of a bounce," I said.

"Only once!" was the reply.

To your marks...

I mentioned that Farokh was a very unorthodox batsman. He would quite easily charge down the wicket to the first ball of the game. He played Glamorgan when Ossie Wheatley was their opening bowler. Farokh had run down the wicket on a number of occasions before Ossie stopped at the end of his run-up and said:

"I don't mind the chap charging up the wicket to me but I do wish that he would let me set off first."

Reading the English weather

We played against Derbyshire at Blackpool and required 120 runs to win the game on the last innings. It was a gorgeous day with not a cloud in the sky. We had all afternoon plus one over before lunch to make the runs. Farokh opened the batting and was *stumped* in the one over prior to the break. We were livid.

"Why on earth did you do that?" we asked.

With that customary shake of the head he replied with a smile:

"I wanted runs on the board before the rains came."

We lost.

Greetings from Headingley

The first time we took our overseas players, Clive Lloyd and

Farokh Engineer, to play against Yorkshire at Headingley we
felt it would not be right to tell them before the game that this
match was different. Yorkshire versus Lancashire is a private
contest and nowt to do with anyone else. We didn't want to
alarm Farokh and Clive, but they were bound to get a hostile
reception to say the least.

The rest of us were seasoned campaigners. There were
standard procedures to go through once we had deposited our
kit in the dressing room. We would stand on the balcony and
look out towards the popular side. That is where all the stick
and flak would come from. It was the same every year. The
stand would be filling up quite nicely but there would be one
chap sat on his own with nobody within twenty yards of him.
That is where all the barracking would start.

He was there again all right. Bib and braces, boiler suit, flat
cap and a lunch box on his knee. We fielded first. Jack Bond
led us out with Clive and Farokh bringing up the rear. Our
friend was stood on his seat and his voice boomed across the
ground.

"Here they come, the League of Nations, they're all shapes,
colours and sizes, this lot, and what's that at back of t' stumps,
he's not fro' Wigan, I can tell that. Is it a Turk, or wot?"

That started Farokh off.

"Turk, Turk, who's he calling Turk. I'll report that man to
the Race Relations Board."

Now, when Farokh signed for Lancashire he could have had
the pick of most counties. Clubs had been clamouring for him.
We took up our fielding positions with our friend still on his
soap box. Farokh turned to the slips:

"I'm so glad," he said in all seriousness. "that I didn't sign
for this lot!".

Slips, batsmen and umpires collapsed with laughter. The
arrival of Sachin Tendulkar was still a long way off in those
days!

North West Frontier

A comedian friend of mine, Mike King, tells a smashing gag about Farokh. He says that Cedric Rhodes, the former Lancashire chairman, had noted that there were growing hostilities between the countries of India and Pakistan. Cedric went to Farokh and said:

"Is there any likelihood of you having to return home and fight for your country?"

Farokh answered, "Only if the fighting reaches my village. Then I will have to go and protect my wife and children."

"Where is your village?" asked Cedric.

"Altrincham," said Farokh.

LAMB'S TALES

Familiar faces

Allan Lamb invited me to play in one of his benefit matches
and when I turned up in the changing room there were quite a
number of familiar faces although I couldn't put names to
them. At this point I must say that I get embarrassed quickly
and am rather forgetful at times. Everyone started to change
and Allan did the introductions – Lloydy, this is Bill, this is
Andy, this Eric, that is John and here we have another Bill, etc,
etc. They all looked very familiar but still I just couldn't place
them.

I opened the batting with Ray Swan, who I did know because
he played Minor Counties cricket. We had got very few runs on
the board when Ray departed and in came one of the Bills. He
was a very dapper sort of bloke, about 5ft 3ins, around 50 years
old, and when he was changing I remember all his kit came out
of brand new wrappers. I thought he must have played for
Hampshire because they always seemed to have new kit. He
had a very determined walk to the wicket and he was
brandishing a brand new Duncan Fearnley Magnum bat. I also
noticed that he had a cheroot hanging from the side of his
mouth. I then decided that he might not have played first class
cricket after all. I did all the usual things, met him, told him
there was no swing and very little pace, just play forward, get
some runs on the board and enjoy the game. Sadly, Bill didn't
last very long and we were in trouble at two wickets down for
not so many.

Next man in was Andy, another slightly-built chap, but
immaculately turned out. Again I did the decent thing and
went across to meet him and told him about the pace, swing,
etc. I also mentioned that Bill was a little unfortunate with his
dismissal and looked a touch out of nick.

I also said, "By the way, Bill looked very familiar, who did he play for?"

Andy looked at me dumbfounded.

"Who did he play for?" he said. "That's Bill Wyman, he plays for the Rolling Stones!"

That, I suppose is the forgetful part of the story. The embarrassing bit was having to walk back the length of the pitch thinking to myself, 'If that was Bill Wyman, who is this Andy?'

I didn't have time to ask him because he was out first ball. We were in desperate trouble. Three wickets down in less than 20 minutes. Coming in next was Bill number two. Let me describe him. There is one of these in every team, every office, every business. Good looking was not in it. He looked magnificent even if I say it myself. Beautiful tan, blonde windswept hair, flashing smile, great physique, and very, very well spoken. I couldn't wait to get across to him and tell him about the wicket. When I got there he smelt great too.

"Now come on Bill," I said, "get stuck in. Don't worry about the score. You look just the man for a crisis. I'm backing you to get 50. Oh, and by the way, Andy struggled a bit, but he looked familiar. Who is he?"

"That's Andy Fairweather-Lowe, the lead singer for Amen Corner."

I couldn't resist saying, "Of course, I should have guessed from his batting – wide-eyed and legless!"

Bill did survive the hat-trick – just. He was out two balls later. We were in a hopeless position. Lamby marched in next. I rushed to meet him.

"Have you had your raffle yet," I asked, "because this game is going to finish at 4 o'clock unless someone gets some runs. By the way, Legga, thanks for the invite to play. I can't believe it. Me batting with Bill Wyman and Andy Fairweather-Lowe. That's my era, you know, the Swinging Sixties. Of course I've got all their records. But that good-looking bloke was familiar,

I've seen him before. Who was that then?"

"You will have seen him on the news," Allan said, "that's 'Bungalow Bill' Wiggins."

Well you could have knocked me down with a feather. I had been a great Dynasty fan, particularly Alexis Carrington.

"Not the same guy that has been going out with Joan Collins?" I asked.

"The very same," said Allan proudly.

After he told me that, I stayed a foot from Bill Wiggins for the rest of the day and night but, needless to say, she didn't turn up, which probably means that as well as being embarrassed and forgetful I can count myself unlucky too.

The winning umpire

I had another encounter with A.J. Lamb, but this time it was on the cricket field. The game was Glamorgan versus Northants at Swansea. Ray Julian, the former Leicestershire wicket-keeper, and I were the umpires. People talk about there not being characters in the game, which I think is a complete nonsense. Ray Julian has got a great dry wit and Lamby is just brilliant out there in the middle. He plays it very hard but with a smile on his face and he never shuts up.

Northants were batting and a wicket fell. Lamby was the next man in. He bounced down the steps in front of the pavilion, out onto the pitch with that pugnacious walk of authority. As he got onto the square and within earshot of everyone, Ray Julian shouted across to me:

"Mr Lloyd."

"Yes, Mr. Julian," I replied.

"I bet I get him before you," he continued.

Lamby chuckled and came out with his usual catchphrase:

"What's happening out here. Come on boys, let's have a bit of decorum, hey."

I don't think he got off the mark before one of the Glamorgan seamers rifled him on the shin with a big nip-backer. There was a tremendous appeal from all round. Ray was the umpire at the bowling end. There was a pause, Lamby looked up. There was a smile on Ray's face.

Lamby said, "Oh no, Ray-mond, Ray-mond, no."

Ray replied with "Oh yes, All-an, yes" and gave him out.

As 'AJ' left the arena but still within earshot, Ray shouted across to me:

"There we are, Mr. Lloyd, I told you I'd get him first!"

Flying the flag

On a mischievous note, in the Test Match against Sri Lanka at Lord's in 1988 England were batting, with Sri Lanka out in the field. The two batsman were A.J. Lamb and Robin Smith. The umpires were David Constant and West Indian John Holder. Lamby took a single, trotted down to David Constant's end and said:

"Do you know, Conny, you are the only Englishman out here today."

Cast adrift

I went on a fly-fishing trip with Allan Lamb to Black Monks Fishery at Evesham. Lamby had a favourite fly which he said was a guaranteed killer on any water. It was his tandem dog-knobbler. It looked like a whaling harpoon! It didn't do much killing on that particular day because he launched his first cast into an oak tree and spent most of the afternoon trying to retrieve it.

THE FAST AND NASTIES

First encounters

I suppose the 'Quickies' are the gladiators of cricket, the hired hands who deliver the goods. My first recollections of the 'fast and nasties' must have been back in the early Sixties when Wes Hall was professional at my home town club, Accrington. He took 126 wickets at an average of around four runs apiece. Our wicket-keeper, Jack Collier, needed to be nearly on the boundary with two prime steaks inside his gloves. Wes used to set off from the sight screen, which from Jack's vantage point seemed to be at the other end of town!

Also in the league at that time were Charlie Griffiths, Roy Gilchrist and Chester Watson. There are no prizes for guessing when all the batsmen playing in the League booked their annual holidays! All this, I can promise you, was a shock to the system of a 14/15-year-old, used to the relative calm of schools cricket. On reflection I suppose it all stood me in good stead for the next 20 years or so at Lancashire County Cricket Club.

A private function

It was at Old Trafford that I got my first taste of 'Roses' matches. Lancashire versus Yorkshire games do seem to be private, which is probably confirmed in the age-old story of one spectator turning to another and asking:

"Where's tha' come fro'?"

"Derbyshire," came the reply.

"Well, what's this got to do wi' thee?" was the retort.

Fearsome Fred

As a young teenager I saw Trueman and Statham on opposite sides and remember thinking that the two, together, must have kept some batsmen up all night. 'George' Statham really was greyhound-like – smooth and graceful, lean and hungry. Then there was his 'oppo', F.S. – classic action, extrovert character and fiercely competitive.

Another classic story, which has stood the test of time, was when Fred was totally destroying India in 1952. An Indian batsman was taking ages positioning the sightscreen and the umpire was getting a little agitated.

"Where *do* you want the sightscreen?" asked the umpire.

"Between me and Mr Trueman," was the forlorn reply.

Come one!

More up to date we have, of course, had a whole cluster (or is it battery?) of West Indian quicks, and who from my era can forget the bush telegraph warning that went around the county scene when Andy Roberts first started terrorising 2nd XIs when he signed for Hampshire. No disrespect to Tom Mottram, who operated at the other end from Andy, but there was a terrific scramble by batsmen to bat at his end.

The Bird that flew the coop

Joel Garner used to have nets at Old Trafford but somehow managed to play for Somerset. Talk about the one that got away! Joel played as professional in the Central Lancashire League and on many occasions would finish with figures like 9-17. Coming at you from 22 feet, or whatever, on damp green tops never was my idea of spending a leisurely afternoon playing cricket after a hard week at the mill.

Sweet dreams

Colin Croft had two spells at Lancashire but never really set the place alight. An ungainly, windmill-type action from wide of the crease was

FOR GOODNESS SAKE LET HIM GET YOU OUT AND LET'S GET SOME SLEEP!

Colin's hallmark, and when the mood took him he would bowl 85 mph leg cutters which bounced shoulder high. Mike Smith, the ex-Middlesex opener, is on record as saying at a Middlesex team meeting, prior to a Gillette Cup knock-out game, that he thought: "Croft will only be medium pace this morning because I've been up all night playing him."

To bowl or not to bowl

However, whilst Colin Croft was at Lancashire, we had great difficulty in getting him to bowl consistently fast. On many occasions he would just amble up to the wicket and bowl at a very military medium pace. It was really exasperating to the rest of the team to have the hired hand, the overseas player, not putting everything in. We tried every conceivable way to get him to fire on all cylinders. Cajoling him, sweet-talking him, upsetting him and in the end, dropping him. It was all to no avail, Colin was his own man.

We played Warwickshire at Old Trafford, and, of course, Dennis Amiss would be opening the batting. I was captain at the time and got the lads together before we went out to field on the first morning the game, just to get everybody gee-ed up and specifically to say to Colin that he should give Dennis a rough time and shake him up a bit with the new ball.

Dennis and I had just returned from the Thomson-Lillee tour and so were in no great shape for another salvo from the quickies. We walked out on to the field and I turned to Colin with clenched fists and said:

"C'mon, Col lad, stick it up him and let's have it fast and bouncy."

His reply was staggering.

"I'm not bowling at all today, man," he said.

I was flabbergasted.

"What do you mean, you're not bowling today?" I raged. "Are you injured?"

"No, man," he replied. "I only know after I have stepped on to the grass, if I want to bowl or not, and today I am not bowling."

I tried the captain bit, the stripes and all that.

"I will decide whether you are bowling or not."

Did he bowl? Of course he did. The only problem was that my Mum could have bowled quicker!

The ultimate challenge

When we came to play Yorkshire at Old Trafford I dearly wanted Colin to do the business, and again got the lads together the night before the game. The chat was specifically aimed at Colin as I said:

"Tomorrow we are playing against the best player in the world, Geoffrey Boycott. He eats quick bowlers for breakfast. Never mind your Greenidges, your Richards, and your Lloyds. This bloke is the best, and on this wicket I can't see us getting him out."

The morning after, Colin was at the ground very early for him, but, of course, Geoff was already out in the nets having a knock. Colin walked onto our dressing room balcony and looked at all the Yorkshire players.

"Which the man Boycott?" he asked.

I sensed that he might mean

business today.

"That's him with the cap on down there," I replied.

This is the scorecard of the game. As you can see, I think Colin was trying to prove a point. He bowled unbelievably quickly.

Bless you!
Colin always fielded at fine leg at Old Trafford in front of the Lady Subscribers' Stand. He had a terrible habit of blowing his nose onto the ground without using a

handkerchief. Numerous complaints came into the club and, as captain, I was called into a meeting to discuss the problem. The outcome was hilarious. It was decided that Colin should field at third-man in front of the popular side.

A matter of respect
Malcolm Marshall will,

LANCASHIRE vs. YORKSHIRE
at Old Trafford on 4th, 6th, 7th June
Toss : Lancashire. Umpires : D.J. Constant and B.J. Meyer
Match drawn

Lancashire

B. Wood	c Johnson b Stevenson	5
D. Lloyd	c Bairstow b Robinson	33
H. Pilling	c Lumb b Cope	31
F. Hayes	c & b Stevenson	90
J. Abrahams	not out	101
J. Simmons	not out	2
J. Lyon		
R. Ratcliffe		
C. Croft		
R. Arrowsmith		
P. Lee		
Extras		8
TOTAL	(for 4 wkts dec)	270

YORKSHIRE

G. Boycott	b Croft	0
R.G. Lumb	b Lee	0
C.W.J. Athey	b Croft	5
J.H. Hampshire	b Croft	10
C. Johnson	c Lyon b Lee	3
D.L. Bairstow	not out	27
G.A. Cope	c Arrowsmith b Croft	8
G.B. Stevenson	not out	0
S. Oldham		
A.L. Robinson		
M.K. Bore		
Extras		12
TOTAL	(for 6 wkts dec)	65

YORKSHIRE	O	M	R	W	O	M	R	W
Stevenson	18.2	2	61	2				
Robinson	30	11	63	1				
Oldham	9.4	3	28	0				
Cope	36	13	81	1				
Bore	6	0	29	0				

LANCASHIRE	O	M	R	W	O	M	R	W
Croft	12.3	4	40	4				
Lee	8	4	8	2				
Simmons	3	3	0	0				
Arrowsmith	1	0	5	0				

FALL OF WICKETS

	LAN	YOR	LAN	YOR
1st	6	1		
2nd	62	6		
3rd	78	17		
4th	246	18		
5th		39		
6th		64		
7th				
8th				
9th				
10th				

WHAT'S YOUR BLOOD GROUP, MAN...?

perhaps, be acknowledged as the best of the cluster of West Indians, and who can argue. He really has come on a bomb since his early days at Hampshire. He is a credit to the game and a great example to young aspiring fast bowlers. He is great to talk to about fast bowling. He is always looking to improve and never afraid to experiment in the nets and then introduce something new to his armoury out in the middle. I might add that the 'something new' is usually in the region of 90 mph.

I had one hilarious moment whilst batting against 'Macko'. I was playing back consistently, and going further and further back. In fact I might have been behind the stumps. He came down the wicket and said:

"You are going back further at your end than I am at mine."

"That's because you are very fast, sir," I said. "You don't mind me calling you sir, do you?"

Quietly destructive

I am sure most players would not disagree that Michael Holding was the nicest bloke you could play with or against. 'Whispering Death' was his nickname on the circuit because they reckoned he was so light on his feet that you couldn't hear him coming. I think 'Exocet' would have been nearer the mark. You could see him coming but there was not a lot you could do about it.

Michael had just one season with Lancashire in 1981, and one game sticks in my mind. We played Somerset at Old Trafford in early May and decided to take them on on a green bouncy wicket. We had Holding, Paul Allott and Clive Lloyd; they had Ian Botham, Viv Richards and Joel Garner. I think the rest of us were just the supporting cast. There had been a big build up to the game in the press. It was billed as the Battle of the Big Guns. It was also reported that the Somerset and former England opener Brian Rose, would be wearing new spectacles.

Michael was playing for Rishton in the Lancashire League at the time and, therefore, played midweek matches for Lancashire. Jack Simmons, myself, Graeme Fowler and Bernard Reidy all lived in the same area and invited Michael out for a drink on the eve of the game. He pondered for a while before saying:

"No thanks, man. I will have an early night. We have a big game tomorrow and I look forward to playing against my countrymen, Viv and Joel and smashing Rose's new specs!"

A friendly gesture

The game was a cracker and in the end Somerset won by 33

runs. The wicket got quicker and quicker and bouncier and bouncier. Our opening bowler and number eleven batsman, Peter Lee, was a good friend of Joel Garner's. 'Leapy' was no batsman and Joel would always pitch the ball up to him. He would play a couple of eccentric drives, Joel would laugh and then he would bowl a fast straight yorker which would always clean up poor Leapy. The first innings went exactly like that. The scorecard read 'P.G. Lee b Garner 9'.

The second innings was quite different. Lancashire were left to score 154 runs to win the game on what was now a very sporty wicket. We were not doing too well with Botham and Garner running through the side like a dose of salts. Nevertheless, at the fall of the ninth wicket we were 121 requiring just the 33 to win. Leapy rose from his seat in the dressing room to start his long walk out to the middle. We noticed that he did not have his protective helmet. Someone said:

"Better wear a helmet, Leapy, this is serious."

"No," he said, "Joel's my mate, he will pitch it up to me."

"Well, he hasn't up to now, not in this innings," came the reply, "and we do only need 33. You had better put this on."

Still protesting, Leapy walked out with the helmet under his arm. He was still having great difficulty getting it onto his head when he got out to the crease. At that time, the helmets had a perspex-like visor with half-inch diameter holes drilled in them to allow air to circulate and to stop them from steaming up. There was a three inch gap between the top of the visor and the neb of the helmet which the batsman looked through.

Leapy thought you looked through the holes in the visor.

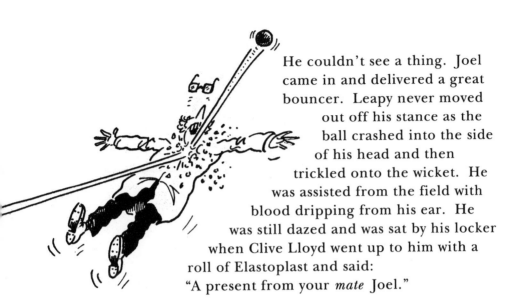

He couldn't see a thing. Joel came in and delivered a great bouncer. Leapy never moved out off his stance as the ball crashed into the side of his head and then trickled onto the wicket. He was assisted from the field with blood dripping from his ear. He was still dazed and was sat by his locker when Clive Lloyd went up to him with a roll of Elastoplast and said: "A present from your *mate* Joel."

Curtley sees red

Curtley is just another in the production line of West Indian fast bowlers, and he is very quickly becoming one of nature's laxatives on the cricket field, especially from 22 yards. What Curtley says, goes. If he says it is Friday, then it is Friday. If he says it is Christmas, then we are all singing carols.

Tim Crowe, formerly of the TCCB marketing department, was compiling the pen-pictures of the West Indies touring team for the Cornhill brochure. All the usual stuff about favourite food, favourite singers, etc. He happened to ask Curtley what was his favourite soccer team.

Curtley replied, "Crown paints, man."

A baffled Tim Crowe shrugged his shoulders, scratched his head, and wandered off. It all became clear when he was watching the soccer highlights on TV that night and saw the team in red come out of the tunnel. It was Liverpool. Who were their sponsors at the time? CROWN PAINTS!

Doing him a favour

Other quickies spring to mind. In another 'derby' game, Notts versus Derbyshire, I was standing at the bowling end for the first over of the game from Devon Malcolm to Chris Broad. The first ball was a quick bouncer which hit Chris on the forearm. The second, another bouncer, flew over his head. The third, yet again a bouncer hit him in the middle of the back. The rest of the over could best be described as short of a length.

Officially I should have called Devon for intimidatory bowling but, whether it was because it was early morning or knowing that Dev has poor eyesight and can only see about 10 yards in front of him, I decided to let it go. My strategy was to go to meet him before the start of his next over, to take his sweater and to tell him to space out the bouncers. I duly went down to third man to meet him and said:

"Hey, big man, come on, pitch it up. I know the bouncer is part of your armoury but don't overdo it. I'm starting to get interested. Are we on

the same wavelength?"

He thought for a minute before he said,

"No, man – I don't like that Broad."

I was getting agitated by this time and said:

"Well, that's the wrong answer, big man. Do it again and I will call you for intimidation."

At this, Devon, burst into laughter and said:

"You're new to this aren't you. I always hit Broady early on to get the cobwebs out of his eyes."

After that he was as good as gold.

Through a glass darkly
Still with a Derbyshire theme, mention must be made of their European import Ole Mortensen. The big Dane breathes fire and brimstone everywhere he goes. The lads reckon that when he attends a club function in the evening, instead of putting 'carriages at midnight' on the menu they put 'longboats at 11 pm followed by an hour's rape and pillage' just to make him feel at home. Another quickie with a huge physique, he is a very good performer with the ability to move the ball away from the bat, but he doesn't half keep the umpires on their toes.

There are many stories about him, in one or two of which I was directly involved. In one match against Northants at Derby he was bowling at Allan Lamb on a helpful wicket. After Michael Holding had cleaned up Wayne Larkins and Robin Boyd-Moss, Ole, or 'Stan' as they call him, after the ex-Blackpool and England centre forward, bowled an absolute 'jaffa' at Lamby, which pitched off-stump, bounced and left. It really was a beauty and deserved a wicket. Stan thought so anyway.

Although Lamby was not in the same parish as the ball, Stan

THIS WAY, OLE...

let
out this
enormous
appeal which
carried him down
the wicket, past Lamby
all the way to Bernie
Maher, the wicket-keeper who
had caught the ball. He
proceeded to indulge in a high-five
with Bernie and the four slips until he
realized that Lamby was still stood there. By this time he was a
good 40 yards away from me. He appealed again. I had to put
my hands to my mouth, megaphone style, and shout back to
him,

"HE'S NOT OUT."

He stomped all the way back up to me muttering in Danish
all the way. Now, when I umpired I wore 'Dennis Taylor-like'
glasses which were photochromatic (they looked darker when
the sun was out). Stan took my glasses off and in Anglo-Danish
said:

"Are you in there, ump?"

I said, "Aye, and I can see all I need to with these on. Here, you try 'em."

And he did! He bowled the next ball with them on.

Three's a crowd

As with most players Stan was not *au-fait* with the finer points of the Laws of the game. He came out to bat in one game with a runner. The opposition were Leicestershire. The law regarding a runner quite clearly states that at all times the injured batsman *and* his runner, in order to avoid being run out or stumped, must *both* be in their ground. That is, if the injured batsman was stood in his ground and the runner ventured out of his, for whatever reason, whilst the ball was in play, the injured batsman would technically be out if the wicket was broken by the fielding side. Clear? Well, anyway, Stan, who batted number eleven, mainly because there are not twelve in a team, was on strike. He played quite a good looking shot and called for a single. It was all very well for him to call the single but he had to stay where he was and let his runner do the running. But Stan set off as well. So we have Stan running, his runner running, the non-striker running and the umpires in fits. The single was quite easy. All three made their ground quite comfortably. Peter Willey, the old pro, had watched all this with great interest from his fielding position at gulley with his arms folded and legs crossed. He shouted across to mid-off, who had fielded the ball:

"Throw the ball to this end."

Mid-off duly did. Wicket-keeper Phil Whitticase took the ball next to the stumps.

"Take the bails off," instructed Willey.

Whitticase did.

"How is he?" enquired Willey to the umpire, Mervyn Kitchen.

Merv promptly lifted his finger and said:

"He's out", and pointed to Stan who was by now way up at

the other end, and had been there for quite some time. Stan was flabbergasted and again in Anglo-Danish said:

"Out, me out. I am in, he is in and he is in. We are all in!"

"Yes," shouted Merv, "but you should be in at this end!"

More Danish muttering as Stan and runner departed.

Perhaps not!

There have been times, since retirement, when I have really fancied a piece of the action. I was umpiring at the Oval – Surrey versus Somerset. It was a gorgeous day, not a cloud in the sky, and the wicket was a Harry Brind 'special', rock hard with not a blade of grass in sight. I really did fancy a knock. Surrey bowled first and, of course, Sylvester Clarke loosed the first salvo. In fact he inflicted severe damage to Jon Hardy's helmet – twice in quick succession! It was then that my enthusiasm for a knock started to wane. Perhaps I should leave it to the lads!

Judegment Days

THE MAN IN THE MIDDLE

One of the first games I umpired was Somerset versus Glamorgan at Taunton. I was really looking forward to the game mainly because Viv Richards was playing. I had played against him many times and invariably he would get a big hundred – in simple terms he would hit it and I would fetch it. It would be different umpiring. For one thing someone else would fetch it. I would just be stood there.

A simple answer

I looked at the wicket in the morning and saw that it was rock hard and green. I thought that Viv might have his work cut out on this track. I needn't have worried. He scored a hundred in 48 deliveries. He had been and gone by 12.55pm during the morning session with 103 to his name. The opening attack for Glamorgan was more than useful. Ezra Moseley, the West Indian paceman, and Greg Thomas, the then England opening bowler, who really did have genuine pace.

I remember Viv came in at the fall of the first wicket. No helmet, no arm guard, no chest pad, just the West Indian cap. A very proud man. He got to the wicket, played a couple of shadowed defensive shots and said:

"Hi, Bumble, man. It's a good day for batting."

Greg bowled him a beauty which beat the outside edge at a very tidy pace. He did it again with the next ball. He then said to Viv, something like:

"It's red and it's round, boyo," hinting to Viv

that he wasn't seeing it too well.

The next delivery was equally as quick but slightly overpitched. Viv laced into it and I didn't need to look where the ball had gone. The noise that it made on the bat told me it had gone a l-o-n-g way. It disappeared over my head, over the big covered stand behind me and we all heard thedistinct plop

as it landed in the River Tone. Now it was Viv's turn. He came down the wicket and said to Greg:

"You know what it looks like. You go and look for it."

The one that got away
I turned up at Worcester to umpire a Benson & Hedges game and Ian Botham came into our room. We are both keen fly fishermen and we had a good long chat about our recent catches and the inevitable ones that got away. Ian was very friendly and helpful and invited me for a day's fishing on a prime stretch of water on the Wye. He also left the Shakespeare catalogue and told me to pick out what I wanted and he would sent it along to me. Brilliant, I needed a new rod, and a reel, keep-net, waders, flies... He left me with the words:

"I'll see you in the middle."

The game got under way and after the opening salvo from Neil Radford and Graham Dilley, 'Both' came on to bowl – my end of course. Now one-day matches have their own regulations, particularly with regard to wides. Both's first delivery was a definite loosener which drifted down the leg side. I immediately called and signalled 'wide ball'.

"It's a what?" said Both indignantly as he spat on the wicket and stood there with his hands on his hips.

"It's a wide," I said, "He couldn't have reached that with a clothes prop."

"Clothes prop, eh?" he said walking back past me to his bowling mark, "you had better get one of those for your fishing because you will get no tackle from me."

Do you know, I check the post every day and still nothing has arrived.

True colours
When Steve Waugh, the Australian Test player, was professional for Nelson in the Lancashire League and played mid-week

county cricket for Somerset, he obviously did his homework and found out that I also played in the League for Accrington when I was not umpiring on the county circuit.

I *was* umpiring the game Surrey versus Somerset at the Oval. Sylvester Clarke, the West Indian quickie, was operating from my end on a really true bouncy wicket. At the time 'Silvers' was the most feared of all the 'fast and nasties' on the circuit, and on this particular day was bowling like lightning. Two wickets went very quickly which brought Steve Waugh to the crease. He immediately started 'chatting me up' or 'getting me on his side', so to speak – familiar lines like:

"Lovely day, ump."

"Yes, lovely day," I replied.

Clarke was still bowling.

"You play in our league, don't you?" he asked.

"Yes," I said, "at Accrington."

"Good league," said Steve.

"Yes," I said.

Clarke was still bowling.

Then he turned to the cricket.

"Quick wicket, ump," Steve said.

"Pacey, very pacey," I replied.

Clarke was still bowling.

"The black guy's sharp," he said.

"Very," I replied.

I thought to myself, 'he's very affable and polite for an Aussie, they don't usually pass the time of day with anyone when they are batting'.

At that point Ian Greig, the Surrey captain, took Silvers off after a very hostile spell lasting about one and a half hours. Steve noticed this and said:

"The black guy is off. He bowled well."

"Yes," I said, "impressive spell."

After three overs Ian Greig had a re-think and shouted to Clarke,

"Silvers, just give me another three from this end."

On hearing this the true Aussie surfaced in Steve Waugh.

"Jeez, they're bringing that big black bastard back again!" he shouted down the wicket to his partner.

'Now that is more like an Aussie', I thought.

A sound decision

Warwickshire versus Glamorgan at Edgbaston and I was standing with Barry Meyer. Allan Donald, the South African paceman, was bowling to that champion Welshman, John Hopkins. He bowled a particularly quick rising delivery which Hopkins fenced at, and there was a big appeal as wicket-keeper Humpage took the ball. 'Hoppy' stood his ground, but as far as I was concerned he had nicked it and so I gave him out. He shook his head as he passed me and said:

"Sorry about that, Bumble, but it hit my shirt on the way through."

I wandered across to Barry and mentioned what Hoppy had said.

"He must have a box of matches in his pocket," he said, "because it sounded very woody to me!"

Royal approval

The Centenary of Cricket in Wales at Sophia Gardens, Cardiff resulted in a friendly game of Glamorgan versus Gloucestershire. The Patrons of both teams respectively were the Prince and Princess of Wales. Both teams and officials would be introduced to the royal couple midway through the game. The moment arrived and the teams were lined up as per the rehearsal earlier in the day. I was one of the umpires for the game and was lined up alongside Paul Romaines, the Geordie batsman for Gloucestershire. Prince Charles came by and asked,

"Are you the referee?"

"Well, yes, sort of, sir. I'm here to see that there is a sense of fair play," I replied.

Princess Diana followed and, being a cricket aficionado, commented:

"Ah, you must be the umpire, it must be jolly hot out there today in that long white coat."

"Yes, ma'am," I said, "perhaps we should call it off and pop down to the pub."

"Quite, quite," she said and moved on to Paul.

I couldn't help overhearing the next conversation.

"I believe I am to have my picture taken with the team," said the Princess.

"Yes, ma'am," said Paul, "will you have the gear on, ma'am?"

"I don't think I would look very good in the gear," she replied.

"Why, aye, ma'am, I'll bet you do!" Paul exclaimed.

ESSEX MEN

During my umpiring days I enjoyed some memorable days observing the fortunes of Essex.

When you're down...
Essex versus Hampshire at Portsmouth saw Geoff Miller, the then Essex off-spinner, bowling to Chris Smith, the Hampshire opening batsman. It was strongly rumoured on the circuit that Geoff had not taken a Championship wicket for over a month. He went round the wicket and drew Smith down the track. Chris hit a firm drive which was airborne and going towards Don Topley at mid on. Could this be the first for a month?

Geoff turned just in time to see Don struck on the chest by the ball. He then grasped at it – and missed. As the ball was on its way to the ground he tried to flick it back up with his foot but only succeeded in kicking it back past Geoff and up the track where it came to rest at Chris Smith's feet. Chris politely walked down the wicket and handed the ball back to the bowler with a consoling:

"Bad luck, Geoff."

Sorely tempted
During the same game I thought that it was too good to be true for me to have got through three days on the same field as Alan Lilley, the Essex batsman, without suffering some sort of physical pain. The Essex boys will tell you that when 'Lill' gets that glazed look in his eyes it is time to retire because, as they say, the lift does not go up to the top floor, or he is a sandwich short of a picnic, and so on.

During the last afternoon of the game, Lill was batting

against Rajesh Maru, the Hampshire spinner. All the fielders were round the bat in catching positions and so I moved in very close at square leg to make sure I could see the popping crease, and

BLOODY HELL, BUMBLE, THAT WAS A CERTAIN FOUR !

generally get a close-up view of what was happening. He suddenly swept the ball like a tracer bullet and I had no chance of getting out of the way. The ball hit me straight on the breast pocket of my umpire's jacket. My light meter was smashed to bits, my fountain pen disintegrated, all the ink ran out onto my shirt, I dropped my six counters and could only find five.

'Is there no end to Lill's talent', I thought. Malcolm Marshall was bowling at my end and it did cross my mind to say, "Just hit him on the leg, Macko, and he's gone."

Expert advice

In another Essex match against Cambridge University, the University captain, Archie Cottrell was bowling his slow left-arm stuff to Graham Gooch who kept despatching the ball with monotonous regularity into the adjoining tennis courts, where the participating players had to abandon the game for their own safety. After yet another Cottrell delivery was on its way to court 3, he turned to me and said:

"Umpire, you used to purvey a little left-arm spin, did you not. Have you any advice you can give me at this juncture?"

"Well. Archie, you can make one or two or them bounce for a start," I replied.

Over-trained

I was stood on the balcony at Chelmsford prior to a game, when Ray East, the Essex 2nd XI captain at the time, was taking the junior players on a training run *à la* Graham Gooch. I guessed that Ray wasn't really into punishing training schedules when he looked up at me and said, "Bumble, if they ever find anyone who can hit the ball three miles, this lot will fetch it back."

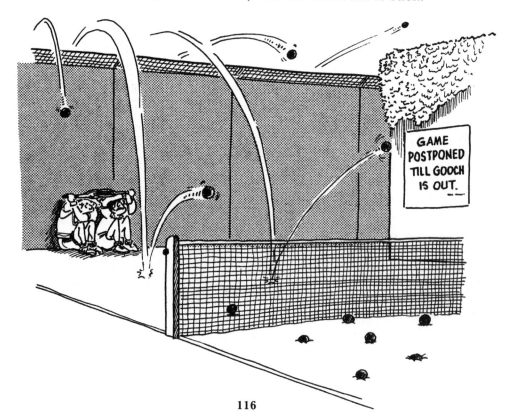

KEEPING THE PEACE

Confrontations are very few and far between on the cricket field but during a six hour day there is bound to be a difference of opinion somewhere along the way. I really enjoyed umpiring and the job itself threw up some very amusing incidents. Apart from making the obvious decisions, I always saw it as my role to get on the same wavelength as the players and just let the game flow. There would, of course, be many flashpoints during a six-hour day and it was my job to defuse the situation quickly, without the public really knowing there was a problem.

Divine intervention

From time to time players do get disappointed and vent their feelings. None more so than Surrey's giant West Indian, Tony Gray. The game was Middlesex versus Surrey at Lord's. The London 'derby'. A great game. I was 'standing' with my back to the pavilion and directly in line with the Committee. I knew that Sir George 'Gubby' Allen was in there, and he was using the resident binoculars that have been in there for as long as I can remember. They are enormous. They stand on a tripod and would be a suitable acquisition for Jodrell Bank. Gray was bowling from my end to John Carr and rapped him on the pads. He let out a great appeal, with arms pumping aloft, running backwards down the wicket and still appealing. I just didn't fancy it. It may have gone over the top or just past leg stump so I quietly said:

"He's not out."

At this Gray dropped to his knees, shouted "Oh, Jesus!" and started thumping the pitch with his fists. I quickly moved from my position behind the stumps, walked down the wicket and tapped him on the shoulder. He looked startled as I said:

"What the bloody hell do you think you are doing? If you do

117

that every time I say 'not out' there is going to be no pitch left
to play on."

Big smiles all round as Ian Greig, the Surrey skipper, came
trotting up from second slip.

"Have we got a problem, Bumble?" he beamed. "Don't worry
about our quickie, he just gets a bit emotional."

"You make sure he gets emotional in the dressing room,' I
said, "and not our here. It's no good him shouting 'Oh, Jesus!'.
You can tell him that God is behind us with those binoculars
and he oversees the lot of us."

In deep trouble

In a match at Derby against Worcestershire there was a good
battle going on between Ole 'Stan' Mortensen and Graeme
Hick. Stan had bowled quite beautifully at Hick, just outside
off stump and moving the ball around from a full length. I was
umpiring at square leg and noticed Kim Barnett, the
Derbyshire captain, manoeuvring Alan 'Jack' Warner squarer
and squarer on the long-leg boundary. It was obvious that they
were setting Hick up for a bouncer but, of course, without him
knowing. Suddenly Stan banged one in. Graeme went for a
hook and the ball soared towards Jack at long leg. Stan had
sprung the trap.

"Catch him, Jack, catch him, catch him!" shouted Stan.

You could have heard him at Trent Bridge, never mind
Derby. In short Jack never got a touch. He fell over and made
a hopeless mess of the chance and Hick ran three into the
bargain. This was all too much for Stan. He shouted

"You shithouse, Jack," which must have carried to Edgbaston,
and then proceeded to chase him round the boundary with Kim
in hot pursuit trying to calm him down.

Dirty Ole

When 6ft 4ins and 14st Stan Mortensen had a difference of
opinion with 6ft 4ins and 15st David Smith – formerly of Surrey,

Worcestershire, Surrey again and presently Sussex – it was obvious, as they confronted each other in the middle of the pitch eyeball to eyeball, that they were not discussing the price of fish. The whole affair looked to be getting really nasty when all the fielders in the immediate area collapsed in fits of laughter. Stan had obviously been watching too many Clint Eastwood films because he said in that broken Danish accent with the high-low inflections:

"Come on, punk, make my day."

Apparently it did not come out quite the way Clint would have said it.

Leave it to the experts

David Smith has the reputation of being a real hard man and not without justification. I certainly would not like to put a six to a seven on the domino table against him. He does have a fair bit to say on the field, but I am sure it is just a wind-up to get the bowlers agitated.

Nigel Plews, an exceptionally good umpire and former Detective Sergeant with the Nottinghamshire City Police Fraud Squad, and I were umpiring the game Middlesex versus Worcestershire at Lord's. Smithy opened the batting and received a ball in the first over from Norman Cowans which rapped him on the knee roll. There was a big appeal from Norman and from behind the wicket. Umpire Plews gave it not out. Smithy never moved but weighed up where the ball had hit him in relation to the stumps. He suddenly shouted down the wicket to Cowans:

"'Ere I'm not having that. Appealing for them. Go on f... off back up there."

I started to back pedal slowly at square leg. I don't want to hear any of this. Smithy

is a big lad after all. Leave it to Nigel, with his background he
is better equipped than me at dealing with things like this, I
thought. It got worse. Mike Gatting, as captain of Middlesex,
was keen to protect his bowler from the verbal assault and
trotted up from second slip in that pugnacious style of his.

"Did you say something to my bowler, then?" he said to
Smithy.

"And you can clear off, as well, you little git. Go on, f... off."

I decided to retreat further. Nigel decided enough was
enough and walked across to me slowly in that assured way that
policemen have.

"Did that batsman say something then?" he asked.

"No, I don't think so," I replied.

"Thank you, Mr. Lloyd. I didn't hear anything either."

He walked all the way back to his position behind the stumps
and said:

"If we have all finished with oratory, can we proceed with the
business gentlemen."

Anything for a quiet life.

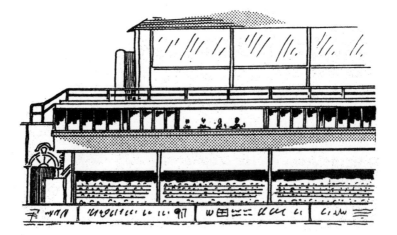

GAMESMANSHIP

In international cricket there is much huffing and puffing, accusations and innuendo, about players tampering with the ball but local club and league players are probably baffled as to what all the fuss is about. Certainly throughout the Lancashire leagues seam picking is a vital part of the game. I recall opening the batting in one game when there was some delay in the bowler commencing his run-up for the first ball of the match. I could see that he was busy working on the ball and I asked the umpire if there was a problem? The umpire replied that Jack was just picking the seam to make the ball move about a bit more! I might add that Jack was a tax inspector. Shame on him.

The trouble with the game these days
I recently had lunch with a current County opening bowler and asked him point blank if he picked the seam. He prodded his peas around his plate for a while before declaring, despondently, that nowadays there was no seam left to pick.

If you believe that!
There has always been gamesmanship and bending of the Laws of the game by players, and even in the first-class game the clever ones can get away with it. It is the umpires job to be ever vigilant and to see that there is a sense of fair play at all times. Easier said than done. Law 42 relates to Unfair Play. Interfering with the condition of the ball Is top of the list. A player must not lift the seam or apply any artificial substance to the ball as it gives an unfair advantage by making the ball do all sorts of crazy things. There was a memorable time out in India when John Lever, the England pace bowler, was pulled up for having what looked like a ton of vaseline around his eyebrows

'to keep the sweat out of his eyes'. Nice one, nice one.

Other tall tales

Brian Statham was a master at picking the seam and was able to do it with the ball in just one hand. It is quite easy to get away with, really. If you know the ropes there are stock excuses which can leave the umpire without a leg to stand on. For instance, if an umpire suspects someone of interfering with the ball he will bring it to the attention of the fielding captain. If he is shrewd the fielding captain will hotly dispute the allegation with excuses like:

"Bill has just trodden on the ball and his studs must have lifted the seam"

or

"It's hit the boundary boards a couple of times which has probably roughed the seam up a little".

The umpire might say:

"I'll have a look again in ten minutes, make sure that the seam is flat."

122

No problem. The game carries on with the same ball and without the umpire having to change it for a ball of much inferior quality, as the Law states, or, as the players say, 'for a bar of soap'.

"It's a fair cop"

I was umpiring a NatWest game with Barry Leadbetter, the former Yorkshire batsman. It was at Jesmond, between Northumberland and Essex. The Jesmond wicket is a beauty and Essex took full advantage and batted first. They got off to a cracking start with Gooch, in particular, in fine fettle. It is fair to say that the Northumberland opening bowlers never got the ball to move off a straight line. The first bowling change brought on P.C. Graham, a tall fast-medium bowler and after a couple of overs from him the ball started going sideways. Very soon Essex lost three quick wickets. I thought 'either the tide has come in or someone is having a nibble at the ball'. At the end of a P.C. Graham over I asked if I could have a look at the ball and sure enough, not only was the outer seam up like a razor edge, but he had got the centre stitching up as well. I shook my head in a very official manner and said:

"Oh dear, this is not good. Captain, can I have a word? I have reason to believe that one of your players is tampering with the ball," and showed him the evidence.

I was waiting for the usual excuses when the captain, Mike Younger, immediately turned and pointed to P.C. Graham and said:

"It's him. He's always doing it. I've told him before about it."

Barry Leadbetter and I fell about, but recovered enough composure to say:

"Well, I'm afraid you will have to continue with this."

And we produced something that looked as if an Alsatian guard dog had been looking after it for a week.

Alan Lilley was the batsman to strike the first delivery with the 'new' ball. He promptly hit it out of the ground and lost it, so we had to give them back the original one!

A personal confession

I must come clean and admit that I, too, fell foul of the umpires in a similar situation when I was captain at Lancashire. Ken Shuttleworth was the bowler. I was fielding at first slip with Frank Hayes at second. The ball was not swinging and so I asked Frank:

"Do you have any lip ice in your pocket?"

(Lip ice, or lip salve, is a good additive for making the ball boomerang and it is almost undetectable if it's properly rubbed in).

"Yes," said Frank, and so I asked him to put some on the ball.

Unfortunately, he did not have time to rub it in. The ball was returned to Shuttleworth who was by now at the end of his run, probably 50 metres away from me. He shouted down the wicket:

"Hey, I can't grip this. There is some stuff on the ball."

Bill Alley, that great Aussie character and English umpire, was the umpire and immediately asked to see the ball. Now it was my turn for a 'come into the office, and can I have a word.'

Before I could get a word out Bill said:

"Now before you say anything, I have done it all and seen it all. Don't tell me that this ball has chapped lips!"

The last word

On another occasion Bill Alley caught Peter Lee picking the seam. He threw the ball back to him after inspecting it and said:

"If you don't get 7 wickets for 20 runs with a ball like that I will report you to Lord's."

ARTHUR JEPSON

Arthur Jepson was a magnificent umpire and a tremendous character. All the players on the circuit used to look forward to him standing in one of their matches because there would always be a story to come out of it. Here are a few of my favourites.

In the umpire's opinion...
Arthur had a deep Nottinghamshire accent and he could not whisper. Everything seemed to boom out. We were in the field at Liverpool, with Arthur standing at square leg and me fielding in that vicinity. The bowler was Neil Radford, who went on to become a formidable bowler when he left Lancashire for Worcestershire. But Neil had a pretty thin time at Lancashire and he would be the first to admit that he did struggle a bit. At that time he had a stuttering, stop-start run-up and bowled from wide of the crease.

On this particular day Arthur was seeing Neil for the first time. His first over was very wayward. A wide, a no-ball, a couple of fours. He was half way down his run-up for the last ball of the over when Arthur turned to me and 'whispered':

"Can this bloke bat?"

The whole game stopped. Neil just stood there with his hands on his hips. I immediately turned to Arthur and, feeling mischievous, said:

"What do you mean, Arthur?"

He was quite oblivious to the fact that the game had ground
to a halt and came back with:

"Well he can't bowl can he? He runs up like he wants a shit."

Basic requirements

The Yorkshire boys tell a story of Arthur, about the time when
the circle of discs was introduced into one-day cricket.
Throughout the duration of each innings you have to have four
fielders within the circle when the ball is delivered. Arthur was
standing in the game and I think Chris Old was the batsman at
the non-striking end. Chris had noticed that the opposition
had only three fielders in their circle and brought this to
Arthur's attention.

"They have only got three in their circle, Arthur," said Chris.

"Well," said Arthur, "what's it got to do with me?"

"I'm sure something has to happen. Either it's a no-ball or
we get some runs added on or something," said Chris.

"Listen here," said Arthur, "I've got six coins in this pocket
and when he bowls a ball I pull one out and put it in this
pocket. I'm watching these lines in front of me to make sure
the bowler doesn't no-ball and then I'm watching the batsman's
pads when they all appeal for lbw and I have to decide whether
he is out or not. If he plays and misses down there, all the
fielders appeal for a catch and I have to decide whether he has
got a touch or not and you're talking to me about discs and
circles – you need eyes up your backside for the game these
days."

As the umpire sees it

Barry Duddleston, the umpire, tells of the time when Arthur
gave him a lift to The Parks at Oxford where they were both
standing in one of the University matches. Arthur had just
taken delivery of a new car, I think it was one of the Volvo
range. Anyway, it was a big car. They were travelling down
Woodstock Road, Oxford, which consists of a bike lane, bus

lane and general traffic lane. The traffic lane was backed up and so Arthur decided to slip into the bus lane for a clearer run. He cannot have been too familiar with the width of the car because he just caught a student on one of those ancient bicycles in the cycle lane.

"Did you hear a noise then, Barry?" said Arthur.

They proceeded further down the road, and lo and behold he nudged another cyclist.

"There's that noise again," he said.

They got to the ground with Barry helpless with laughter as Arthur locked his car and then stood back in admiration at his new vehicle. It was then that he noticed his wing mirror was turned in towards the car.

"Look at that," he said, "fancy having vandals in Oxford!"

Words of encouragement

In another match at Oxford, I was bowling and was half-way through an over when Arthur said to me:

"I hope you don't mind me mentioning this but you are the worst bowler I've ever seen. Fred Price was a bad 'un, but you're worse than him."

Speaking
from
Experience

"MR PRESIDENT, MR CHAIRMAN, DISTINGUISHED GUESTS ..."

It usually starts with a phone-call from someone whose first words are:

"You don't know me..."

That is the signal to get the diary ready because you are going to be asked to speak at a dinner. It could be anyone's dinner. It is really surprising the number of obscure groups who will get together for a celebration. It could be the Slaters' and Tilers' Institute of Cheshire, Lancashire Floor-coverers Association, The Duke of Gisburn's Light Cavalry Eleven's Re-Union Dinner, Harlingden Plunge Bath Attendants' Monthly Meeting, Wellingborough Skin Lifters' Society or the like.

My most bizarre function was the Malayan Water Authority annual bash held at the Old Trafford cricket ground. I think I accepted more out of curiosity than anything else.

After the caller tells me all about his particular function, I ask him a series of questions, similar to a bomb scare procedure, and if the answers do not stack up there is no way that I will be persuaded to attend. I ask things like:

"What time do you anticipate sitting down to dinner? How many speakers will you be having? When will I be on? Who is the MC?", etc.

The majority of dinners are very pleasant affairs but some can be absolute disasters. The seasoned after-dinner speaker will know what to expect as soon as he enters the room and meets the organiser.

Recipes for disaster will probably take the following form: the ticket will say 7.15 pm for 7.45 pm and at 8.30 pm 'the lads' are still attacking the free bar. The MC for the evening says that he is just letting everyone get into the spirit of the occasion. I try, tactfully, to say that maybe time is running short if they are to cram in everything planned on the menu, Chairman's welcome, Grace, two raffles, four speakers, of which I am the last, an auction, President's closing remarks, with a meal crammed somewhere in the middle.

When everyone is eventually seated, an individual with a religious background is called upon to say Grace. The chap has probably attended a funeral recently which qualifies him for the job. The most unusual I heard was by a man who said solemnly:

"For what we are about to receive may the Lord be truly thankful, and never mind the needs of others."

The MC, who I can sense just loves the microphone, then outlines the format for the evening. At this point the mike goes on the blink. I mention this to the MC who says:

"Never mind, lad, you'll just have to shout up a bit."

This is quite a tall order when there are 650 people in the room.

The green pea soup is now served and half of it finishes up on my back. The waitress apologies and I console her by saying:

"Never mind, luv, it'll go well with last week's tomato."

The MC is back again to explain the first raffle:

"Gen'lemen, please. Thank you. Gen'lemen, please, gen'lemen, thank you."

I wonder if I am at the right do and half expect two boxers to make an appearance. There are 23 raffle prizes and our MC goes through them all with full details of those who donated them – a cool 30 minutes.

Main course comes and goes with liberal amounts of wine being served to the top table. I decline as I don't drink before speaking and in any case I am in the car. The MC, who is now on his second bottle, turns to his Chairman and says something which seems to throw doubt on my sexual prowess, then he is on his feet, rather unsteadily, to tell us all about the next fund-raising effort – stand-up bingo. In short, you buy a bingo ticket and everyone stands up. If a number is called which is on your card, you sit down. The last one standing is the winner – simple. The way our MC explains it you would have to be Einstein and Archimedes rolled into one to understand.

After the meal is concluded there is the auction, conducted by a, by then, very inebriated MC whom only Stanley Unwin would understand.

(Stanley Unwin always makes me chuckle and I will never forget the advert that he did for Gale's Honey:

"Gale's Honey is the puriemost of the sunnyglows and the buzz of the hivers with the pollen on the nectars – and it is all up to Gale's." What a classic.)

The time has wandered on to 11.15 pm and the only person that the august gathering has heard is the MC, but it is now time to introduce the first speaker, who needs little or no introduction – nevertheless, he gets one. One by one speakers come and go until, at last, it is my turn. The MC, who by now is absolutely incoherent, announces a 'pee' break mainly because he wants one. A further delay before I am on my feet and, in fact, it is now tomorrow.

I always start with the same line:

"Mr President, Mr Chairman, distinguished guests, gentlemen, 18 handicap golfers, vagrants, vagabonds, tramps, plebs and solicitors, welcome to everyone. I have been here that long I thought that I had already been on..."

I attended a very up-market company dinner and after the meal the Chairman got up and said:

"I hope you have all enjoyed the Thermal Lobsterdor this evening."

SKY SPORTS

It is tremendous fun working for BSkyB on Sky Sports, although it was not very funny on the first day of the 1991 season when we started the Refuge League fixtures at Leicester, where the home side were entertaining Derbyshire. I hesitate before claiming it was a 'Thriller in Manila' and not to be missed. What I will say is that it was a bitterly cold mid-April Sunday afternoon with squally hail showers. The commentary team all had thermals on, along with bobble-hats and mufflers, and anyone sat out watching must have been plain daft. After all *we* were being paid and had to be there.

Beware of prediction
I quickly realised that I was the learner with a large 'L' plate, compared to all the revered names in the commentary box. It was brought home to me during a NatWest quarter final at Worcester when the home team were drawn against Lancashire. Five minutes before tea Worcester lost a wicket. I was doing the summary and it went something like this:

"And that is a bad time for Worcestershire to lose a wicket but, arguably, one of the best players in the world is coming in to bat now, Graeme Hick. He will not be relishing these few balls before tea and Lancashire can go a long way to winning this game if they can remove him quickly. Hick, for his part, will be looking for survival, pushing the odd single and getting down to the non-striker's end...and that is a magnificent six to get him off the mark."

On top of the job
Our producer on Sky Sports, John Nienaber, has a reputation for being a hard taskmaster and not without some justification. He had me helping to rig the camera at the top of Worcester

Cathedral for the high shot of the ground. When I got up there I found that I was surrounded by nothing but fresh air and I must say I am one of those who gets dizzy on a thick carpet! Surely, it must be easier being just a player.

Trouble with the locals

John Nienaber also masterminded the World Cup operation from the Australian end. The coverage was excellent and went really well – until Ballarat.

England played Sri Lanka at Ballarat and the game was not in the schedule of the host broadcaster, Channel 9. Of course, from this end, we had to see England in all their matches and so a local production company was hired for the day – and I mean local. Channel 9 would usually have upwards of twelve cameras, we had only three – one straight at each end and one square at cover/mid-wicket. Mike Gatting presented and in the pre-match interviews he stressed that it was very, very hot and I swear 'Gatt' must have lost a stone just standing out in the middle talking about the pitch. The match got under way and, in our ear pieces back in London, we could hear the director talking to the cameramen out in Ballarat.

After a while John Nienaber called for a shot of the crowd from the side-on camera. No picture came. All that appeared was a shot of the sky with the occasional bird flying past. The conversation then started to get interesting and we turned up the volume in London.

"Camera three, crowd shot," commanded John. "Three, crowd shot – not the bloody clouds – CROWDS – somebody get to three, he obviously can't hear."

A production assistant hot-footed it round to camera three's position and came through with:

"Jeez, boss, three's crook – he's fell over in the heat."

"Well prop the bastard back up again," said John, "we need pictures."

We were hearing everything now as the cameraman was doused with cool drinks and gradually brought round.

"You all right three?" demanded John.

"She'll be right," said the gallant number three cameraman.

A few overs passed by and John called for a shot of the scoreboard from side-on. You've guessed it – he had kettled over again and left us with another shot of the sky.

"Jeez, the bastard's gone again," said the now irate Nienaber.

The perfect answer was found in true 'show must go on' tradition. A production assistant was deployed with a bucket of water and every time it looked as if camera three was about to leave us, the flagging cameraman was doused from top to toe. A hard man that Nienaber.

We get letters

During the World Cup we had lots of letters from the public. Some on the games themselves, some with points of view and some on the wider issues of the game. A chap wrote in to say that he was new to Sky, he had just got his dish and was thoroughly enjoying the day/night cricket. However, he went on:

"I have just seen the England opening batsmen walking out and would like to know if that man Botham really is that big or does my horizontal hold need adjusting!"

Another viewer wrote in on a similar tack saying that he was new and thought that the sports coverage, and in particular the cricket, was excellent. He went on to say that he also enjoyed the adverts and was really getting interested in them. Whilst he accepted that he never missed the first ball of a new over he did, on occasions, miss the end of the adverts and would like to know if they all had a happy ending.

INTERVIEW TECHNIQUE

Don't broadcasters and journalists ask some really dumb
questions sometimes? I remember watching TV one evening
when Mike Gatting appeared, propped up in a hospital bed,
after returning home prematurely from the West Indies for
surgery to his nose after Malcolm Marshall had re-arranged his
face during the first Test match out there. He looked like a
giant panda and the state he was in he was never going to find a
mate. The interviewer's first question was:

"Can you show us where the ball hit you!"

There is a similar story about the lion which escaped from
London Zoo and a number of MCC members were
seen fleeing along the Finchley Road. An anxious
passer-by asked:

"Which way is it headed?"

A breathless member snapped back, "You
don't think we're chasing it, do you?"

Whilst working for Satellite TV I was sent
outside Lord's before the Benson and
Hedges Cup Final to interview the crowd
and to get their thoughts about the game
between Lancashire and Worcestershire.
This type of interview is known in the trade
as vox pops.

The first chap I approached had a beard, long hair, and was dressed in T-shirt and jeans. I approached him and said:

"Good morning sir, how do you think the game will go this morning?"

He looked at me quite nonplussed and replied:

"F... off mate, I'm trying to sell tickets." Cut!

TEST MATCH SPECIAL

Historical fact

During the Old Trafford Test against India in 1990 the Test Match Special team were invited to dinner with the BBC Radio Head of Sport, Leslie Robinson, at New Broadcasting House. It was a super evening with great cricketing tales and anecdotes from everyone. Fred Trueman, obviously a great character and after-dinner speaker was on terrific form, and at one time said in that deep Yorkshire voice:

"I'm the best fast bowler the world's ever seen since the game was invented in the year 1040."

Quite a profound statement, and there was a slight pause until Christopher Martin-Jenkins came back with:

"I'm not so sure about that last statement Fred. I believe that Hereward the Wake had a particularly good spell in 1070."

"Aye, but he weren't as quick as me," said FS.

A prize pair

During the fiasco on the second day of the 1992 Edgbaston Test match between England and Pakistan when only two balls were bowled, Trevor Bailey received a letter from a lady which Brian Johnston read out on Test Match Special. The lady wrote:

"Dear Mr, Bailey,

Your two balls on the Friday were the most expensive I have ever seen ....."

Ferrets by fax
Our Saturday guest on Test Match Special for the same game
was James Judd, the internationally acclaimed classical music

conductor. A number of the team had met James at the Trent Bridge Test match in '91 when we stayed at the same hotel. Brian Johnston, who does these interviews, was not with us and wanted more research and background information about James.

On the Friday evening we had dinner together and 'Johners' was worried about Saturday lunchtime and hoped it would go well. He asked me if I knew anything else about James Judd. I quickly replied that I recalled he supported Aldershot FC. Conversations turned to other things.

The following morning I sent a fax to Johners on BBC headed paper. It went like this:

Additional info on James Judd from Peter McLeod, BBC Radio 3 Presentation.

1. Great supporter of soccer (do not know which team).

2. Recently was guest conductor for the Weetabix-sponsored Icelandic Male Voice Choir.

3. Has rare collection of Japanese bonsai plants.

4. Tastes in music vary from Rachmaninov to Wagner, but also wrote theme music for Clint Eastwood film, 'Any Which Way but Loose' and lyrics for Long John Baldry's Top Ten hit 'Let the Heartaches Begin'.

5. In his formative years he kept ferrets, hence the nickname 'Ratty'.

Johners busily prepared notes on Ratty and rejoiced in knowing that the soccer team was Aldershot, because 'Bumble' had remembered.

After about an hour of writing Peter Baxter imagined that Johners would be opening up with questions like:

"Jolly nice to see you, Ratty, have you brought the ferrets along, sorry about 'The Shots' and do tell us about the Bonsai plants."

Panic set in until Peter said to me:

"Your handwriting is remarkably similar to Peter Mcleod's at

Radio 3 Presentation."

The penny dropped with Johners and if we had been on air we would have had another Brian Johnston/Jonathan Agnew 'leg over' episode on our hands.

Peter Baxter remarked that it was very rare for Johners to be had. A quick look through the records by Bill Frindall confirmed this.

"583-1," he declared to the nation.

Unfortunate observation

This was not the first time Johners had been troubled by ferrets, during one stoppage for rain he was telling the listeners about this and that, and something led him to say:

"It reminds me of a fellow from Heckmondwyke I interviewed who kept ferrets. He was very interesting and it surprised me to know that you should only keep male ferrets down your trouser leg....(long pause)...I suppose females just gobble away...and what a lovely cake we have received from ...."

THE GREAT MAN HIMSELF

Working for BSkyB on Sky Sports has meant I have come up against England's finest, Geoffrey Boycott. 'Boycs' is true to his reputation and calls a spade a shovel. He says what thinks and, of course, the truth hurts from time to time.

Our brief from the Director, John Nienaber, a ruthless but very likeable Australian who manages to do his job brilliantly and keep us all in check, was that the Lancastrian (me) and the Yorkshireman (Boycs), should from time to time engage in a bit of banter.

Winning ways
During one game when we worked together I was lead and Geoffrey was colour. In other words I would add words to the picture with Boycs providing the summary. Kim Barnett opened the batting for Derby with his usual unorthodox, open stance at the crease. The big Aussie fast bowler Maguire opened the bowling for Leicester and rapped Barnett on the inside of the thigh where there was definitely no protection. Barnett hopped about rubbing the painful area furiously and I am sure it brought tears to his eyes.

I happened to say on air that you know the season has started when the ball whacks into your leg in bitterly cold April weather, especially if it hits you on the inside of your thigh.

Boycs paused and waited for the playback before replying:

"Yes, you probably got a lot of those because you were not as sideways on as I was. It never happened to me."

He wins every time. In fact, he has been winning ever since he ran me out in a Test Trial at Hove back in 1973. He shouted "No!" and ran straight past me to where I should have been standing.

IT'S A ROYAL COMMAND FROM GEOFFREY BOYCOTT...

YOU WILL SPEAK AT MY DINNER

Give credit where it's due

Everyone knows Geoffrey Boycott was a great player. He has a reputation as being a dour Yorkshireman but I found him a terrific competitor to play against with a very sharp wit. He rang me on one occasion and asked me to speak at one of his benefit functions. In fact he didn't ask – he told me I would be speaking at the do!

I was introduced as a Lancashire and England cricketer. I did my bit. It went OK, and then the Chairman went into his introduction of our guest of honour. All the thousands of runs, the hundreds, the caps, the tours. It was a magnificent build up. Boycs took the applause and rose to his feet. His first line was a classic:

"Mr Chairman, the previous speaker was introduced as a Lancashire and England cricketer but everyone in the room knows he would never have played for England if I hadn't been injured!"

Too much class

On another occasion, Boycs and I were stood together after a game, just making conversation.

I said, "Have you been scoring many runs lately, Boycs?"

He lifted one eyebrow, as only he can, and said:

"I always score runs."

He then continued:

"But I had a bit of a rough time last week. We were playing Surrey at the Oval. They have got that Geoff Arnold, fast-medium outswingers, bowls off-stump, gets you playing at things that you shouldn't be playing at. I had it all worked out, played it when I should have, left it when I should have. I was just settling in well. He then produced a 'jaffa'. He went wide of the crease and angled the ball into me, it pitched off stump and then started to leave me. I was a bit square on by this time and

was about to leave it when I got a thin edge and was caught behind."

He then paused before coming back with,

"An ordinary player like you would never have touched it."

Geoffrey's cat

The Sky presenter Charles Colvile, or 'Charlie Chan, the Sky man', loves his stints at commentary, and to say he pumps up the volume when a wicket falls or when the ball disappears into Row 6 of C stand is an understatement. He goes absolutely potty. When he first appeared with Geoffrey they were still getting to know each other, with Charlie asking questions like:

"Was this one of your favourite grounds?" or "How many hundreds did you score here?"

Then suddenly a wicket fell and Charlie went into overdrive, which must have tested the sound engineer to the limits,

"BOWLED HIM – GONE – GREAT DELIVERY – GEOFFREY?"

Now, Boycs should have come in at this point with his expert analysis. Instead the viewers got:

"Don't do that, I've heard you before and so has my cat George. Every time you start shouting he runs up the chimney and it's days before he comes down again."

Pink pigeons

Geoffrey, of course, loves to chat about cricket. He loves his golf too, and talks admiringly about the great achievers in other sports. He waxes lyrical about people like Nick Faldo and Bjorn Borg – perfectionists like himself. He also listens and takes an interest in other peoples' hobbies and pastimes. He noticed that Henry Blofeld and Bob Willis talked enthusiastically and

authoritatively about wine. Serious wine – fine wine. Over dinner one evening he asked Henry whether he drank wine *every* night.

"Oh, my dear old thing," started Henry, "when my wife comes home from the office after a particularly awful day at the office we might relax with a rather drinkable claret, and if it has been a really ghastly day we could finish the evening with an even more drinkable glass or two of champagne. Nothing better, my dear old thing.'

Boycs looked at Henry and came back with,

"Well, it's no wonder you keep seeing pigeons and red buses when you're commentating!"

Back-seat Boycott

The Benson and Hedges zonal matches in 1991 saw us at Headingley on a Tuesday followed by Cardiff on the Thursday. Boycs asked me at Headingley if I had a big car.

I said, "Yes, it's a BMW 7 series."

"That'll do, I'll come to Cardiff with you."

I thought to myself, 'I haven't bought any tickets for the raffle but it looks as if I have won first prize.'

We finished at Headingley and set off en route to South Wales. Geoffrey reclined the front seat, put his famous Panama hat over his eyes, his feet on the dashboard and said:

"Wake me up at the hotel."

Some way along the journey, and please don't ask me how, we inexplicably found ourselves in a Tesco car park in Derby. I was doing a three-point turn manoeuvre to get us back onto the road when he woke up, lifted his hat and mumbled:

"Where are we?"

"Tesco's car park, Derby," I said.

He sat bolt upright and started ranting, "TESCO'S BLOODY CAR PARK, DERBY! Derby, what are we doing in Derby?"

"I think we're lost," I said meekly.

"WE are lost – we – it's you that's lost, you thick Lancastrian....etc, etc."

With that he promptly put the Panama back over his eyes and muttered himself nearly back to sleep again. I say nearly because he woke as I stopped at the next petrol station. He was bolt upright again.

"What are you doing now?" he asked threateningly.

"Stopping for petrol," I said. "These things don't run off fresh air, you know."

"Exactly," he retorted, "that's why you should have filled up before we set off."

He banged on and on:

"Preparation, forward planning, attention to detail – it's just like batting. Come to think of it you never did any of that when you were batting. That's why you never got any runs."

With that he bounced out of the car and steamed into the shop area. He picked up a packet of mints and said to the cashier:

"That gormless Lancastrian out there will pay for these – he has got the brains of a chocolate mouse."

When I went into the shop people were tripping over themselves and banging into things and I could hear them saying:

"That's Geoffrey Boycott – Geoffrey Boycott, sat in that car."

I paid for the petrol *and* the mints, and the young chap said:

"It's Geoffrey Boycott sat in that car, isn't it?"

"Yes," I said, "we're on our way to the Benson and Hedges match at Cardiff."

I held my hand out to introduce myself and I said

"My name is ...".

I didn't get any further.

He interrupted me with, "Oh, we know you – you're the chocolate mouse from Lancashire!"

The last word
I always have a go at Boycs saying that, as a bowler, he never got me out but I did him twice. He comes back with the same line every time.

"Aye, but slip caught it between his legs the first time and I had got 135 the second time."

What a memory!

A sentence too far
May 3rd, 1992. Yorkshire versus Nottinghamshire, Sunday League. An historic day for Yorkshire. The first televised game featuring their first-ever overseas player, 19-year-old Sachin Tendulkar, the Indian batting sensation. Our intrepid presenter, Charles Colvile, went hotfoot for an interview with the little master. Sachin was lovely, saying all the right things:

"Great to be here – I always wanted to play county cricket – yes, I think we will do well."

Finally, Charles asked him if he knew much about Geoffrey Boycott. At this the commentators – Lloyd, Blofeld, and Willis – the production crew, the cameramen, the scorers, the studio

people at Sky, all suddenly went very quiet and listened. Sachin beamed and said how great a player Geoffrey was, with a marvellous technique. Amen and hear, hear to that. Perhaps he should have left it at that but he rounded it off by saying:

"Boycott is perfect in everything he does."

Sachin, lad, oh, Sachin. Did you have to say that? You are a great player but there are some things that are better left unsaid!

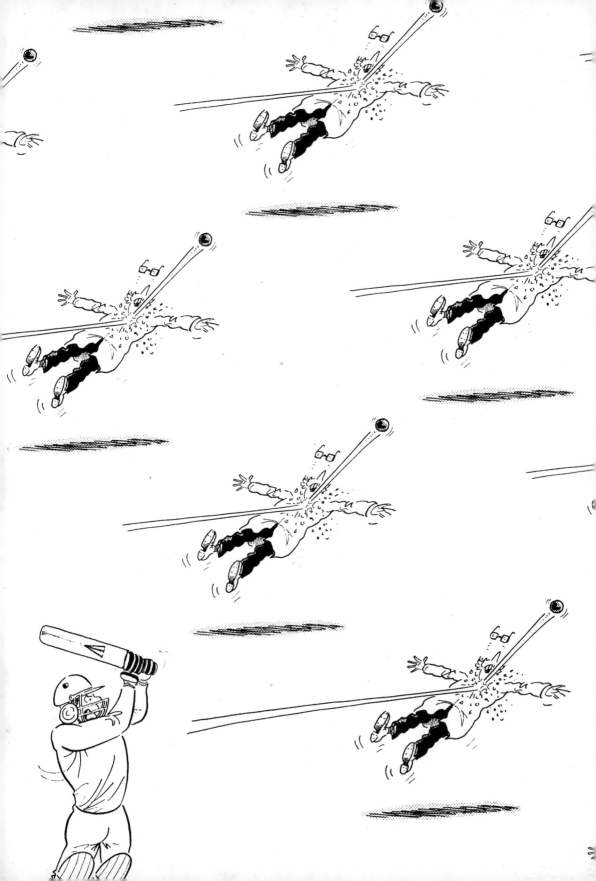